A THOUSAND KISSES

A THOUSAND KISSES

The Letters of Georg and Frieda Lindemeyer
1937–1941

Edited by Christoph Moß

Translated and abridged by Katharina Bielenberg

BLOOMSBURY

First published in Great Britain in 2006

First published in Germany as '. . . *Wir leben doch in Gedanken
nur mit Euch . . .*': *Breife von Georg und Frieda Lindemeyer 1937
bis 1941* by Evangelische Kirche im Rheinland in 2002

Bloomsbury Publishing Plc, 36 Soho Square, London W1D 3QY
A CIP catalogue record for this book is available from the British Library

ISBN 0 7475 8031 6
ISBN-13 9780747580317

10 9 8 7 6 5 4 3 2 1

Typeset by Hewer Text UK Ltd, Edinburgh
Printed in Great Britain by Clays Ltd, St Ives plc

All papers used by Bloomsbury Publishing are natural,
recyclable products made from wood grown in well-managed
forests. The manufacturing processes conform to the
environmental regulations of the country of origin

Dedicated to the Lindemeyer Family

CONTENTS

The Lindemeyer family, 1924.
From left to right:
Georg, Edith, Wolfgang, Eva-Maria and Frieda

Introduction

I never knew my grandparents. Georg and Frieda Linde-meyer, like countless other victims during the Second World War, were killed by the Nazis in 1941.

My mother, Eva-Maria, was sent away to England along with her brother and sister, Wolfgang and Edith, to escape Nazi persecution when they were all still young. They hardly saw their parents during this time, but kept closely in touch through letters. Most of the letters the children sent disap-peared with their parents. But Georg and Frieda's letters to the three siblings remain. They start in 1937, when Edith went away to school in England, and end on the day my grand-parents were deported to the ghetto in Minsk. As historical documents they are enigmatic, but although facts are hard to glean from the letters their human value is deeply apparent.

My aunt Edith kept the letters in her attic, and when she died in 1996 they were handed to my mother. When I first saw the letters, I found them inspirational and frustrating at the same time. Inspirational because they were as close as I could ever get to my grandparents, and closer by far than I had ever been before. They were frustrating, however, because despite being a German speaker I found them

for the most part utterly illegible, as they were written in
gothic script and on the flimsiest of paper.

I decided to have them transcribed and published and
was put in touch with Dr Christoph Moss, a historian
specialising in the National Socialist period. With the
financial support of the Evangelical Church of the Rhineland, Christoph and colleagues of both his and mine set
about the arduous task of transcribing and editing the
letters. The German edition of this book, '*Wir leben doch
in Gedanken nur mit Euch*' ('*We are only thinking of you*'),
was published in 2002. My mother Eva-Maria was very
excited by this project and was certain Edith would have
been as well. She lived to see the German edition in print,*
and died in March 2005, knowing that this English edition
was on its way.

The Lindemeyer story

What sets the story of the Lindemeyers apart is that they
were Jews who had converted to Christianity. Although the
letters themselves communicate relatively little of these
complexities, it does make their story doubly tragic especially as they were never fully supported by the Church.

As in many other countries, German Jewry underwent a
period of assimilation from the late nineteenth century

---

* In fact the last time my mother returned to Düsseldorf was with Wolfgang and
his wife, together with my sister and me, in 2002 to participate in a ceremony at
the Mahn und Gedenkstätte (memorial centre) which marked the publication of
the German book. It was a particularly emotional occasion as the event was
attended by many friends from her school days in Düsseldorf.

onwards. But there was always a lingering threat of anti-Semitism and it was a powerful influence on many Jews. Between 1880 and 1919, for example, the number of Jews who converted to Christianity rose from approximately 11,000 to 25,000, and my grandparents were among those who converted during this period.

Georg was born on 5 August 1887 to a Jewish business-man, Moritz Lindemeyer, and his wife Mathilde in Wuppertal-Elberfeld, near Düsseldorf, in the Rhineland. When Moritz died in 1892, Georg's mother married Georg Hobbie, his business partner. Hobbie was a Protestant and insisted that his stepson be baptised.

Georg Lindemeyer was brought up as a practising Protestant. He was a highly intelligent boy, with an artistic and scholarly bent. His two best friends at school were the future poet and writer Karl Adrian, who was killed in action in 1917, and Gustav Halm, who became a celebrated children's writer and broadcaster. After school, Georg went on to study law at Bonn and Heidelberg universities. Like so many students of that period, he also immersed himself in Philosophy, French (which led to his work as an interpreter in the First World War), History and Classics, and this passion for scholarship would remain with him all his life. Georg finished his studies and in 1912 was apprenticed to the Jewish lawyer and Privy Councillor Arnold Lewinsky in Berlin. It was at his office that he met Frieda, who was Arnold's daughter.

Frieda was born on 24 June 1893 in Berlin to Arnold and Hedwig Lewinsky. She was the second youngest of five children (there are many references in the letters to her sisters, Hanni, Bertha and Erna, and brother Paul). Frieda had been working at the Lewinsky legal practice since 1910 after finishing school in Switzerland.

The couple were married in 1915. Ironically, the Lewinskys disapproved of their daughter marrying a Christian. This prompted Georg and Frieda to move to Düsseldorf, where Georg started up his own legal practice.

Frieda became pregnant shortly after the move to Düsseldorf. But she was told that there was a possibility that she would not survive the birth. This persuaded her to convert to Christianity so that she might be buried with her husband. The child died within a few days, but Frieda's life as a committed Protestant had begun. There are numerous instances of her faith throughout the letters, and she was a pillar of the Church community. There is even a commemorative tablet to the Lindemeyers in their local church in Oberkassel. The next year Frieda had a girl, my mother Eva-Maria, who was born on 21 March 1917. Two years later, Edith was born on 27 April 1919, and Wolfgang followed on 26 December 1922.

Until 1933, the Lindemeyers led comfortable, happy lives at their home in the Salier Strasse in Oberkassel, on the west bank of the Rhine. Theirs was an affluent, church-going household like so many German middle-class families. But at the heart of the family's identity lay its cultural bent. Georg was a prolific writer, and had written novels, poetry, film scripts and literary criticism. They mixed among a highly cultured social milieu and musical evenings or discussions of a literary nature were commonplace. Georg was also a supporter of the Social Democrats and had many friends from the organisation with whom the family would socialise.

I would even hazard to say that Georg and Frieda were keen to disassociate themselves from their roots. My mother and her siblings grew up utterly unaware of being Jewish, for example, and were told of their origins only once the National Socialists came to power.

1933–1939

The stable world the Lindemeyers had built began to fall apart after Hitler came to power in 1933. In 1935, the Nuremberg Race Laws introduced new criteria in the classification of Jews. Included among them were not only those who practised the religion, but also anyone who had at least two grandparents who were Jewish. The family aligned their interests with those of other Christians of Jewish descent through the Paulusbund* but found that, despite this, they were classified by the Nazis as Jews, and therefore subject to increasing persecution.

Georg could not act as a solicitor any more, though he continued practising law in a minor capacity with a dwindling base of clients. The lack of income forced the Lindemeyers to move out of their beloved home in Salier Strasse, and into a succession of ever cheaper rented apartments,

---

* The Paulusbund was founded in 1933, the same year that the National Socialists came to power. The full German name of this organisation is 'Reichsverband christlich deutscher Staatsbürger nichtarischer oder nicht rein arischer Abstammung' or 'League of Christian German citizens of non-Aryan or not pure Aryan extraction'. It is clear from this title that the objectives of the League were to emphasise the German character of its members. Georg Lindemeyer gave several talks to the League on literary subjects.

first at no. 78 Stein Strasse in 1934, then to Cranach Strasse in 1936, and finally to Yorck Strasse in 1938.

The family's principle income now came from selling soaps and cleaning material from the Steinhaus Company, and chocolate from Adler, an arrangement set up by the Hamachers,* who were friends of the family. Wolfgang did the deliveries on his bicycle, and when he left for England in 1937 this source of money dried up. The family were now utterly impoverished, although some financial support was received from the Hamachers and Alfred Cöhn, an uncle of Frieda's.†

Georg and Frieda were forced to think of alternate plans for their children. In 1933, Eva-Maria was working as a secretary, after being forced to leave school at the age of sixteen. There is no doubt she would have gone on to higher education had it not been for laws limiting the number of Jews allowed into it. She later told my sister Carolyn that one of the teachers at her old school, a Miss Hayden, continued to give lessons to her along with the other expelled Jewish pupils, potentially at great personal risk. Georg and Frieda were happy that she stayed in Germany for the time being.

They began to look into getting their two younger children to study outside Germany, given the unlikelihood of them finishing in Düsseldorf. In 1937, they arranged for

---

* When Frau Hamacher was ill in the 1920s it was Frieda who supported her financially and emotionally. In turn the Hamachers supported the Lindemeyers as the Nazis took power, including finding them work and protecting them on Kristallnacht.

† Alfred Cöhn was the brother of Hedwig Lewinsky, Frieda's mother. He was a prominent professor of Chemistry and specialised in photography.

Edith to be sent to England to attend Stoatley Rough School in Surrey.* The letters in this book start from this point. Edith was eighteen years old at the time. She finished at Stoatley Rough and then moved on to work at the St Mary's Home for Disabled Children in Horam, Sussex. Throughout her adult life she took great pleasure in teaching young children, though she was to have no children of her own. I remember Edith as being a loving and very emotional person, but who was never in good health. I have no doubt that the period of separation from her parents at such an early age left its mark on her.

Wolfgang followed Edith to England in the same year to start at the Magdalen School in Brackley at the unimaginably young age of fourteen. His schooling was financed by the Inter-Aid Committee. By 1939 Inter-Aid were no longer prepared to pay for Wolfgang's education (this would be a cause of much anxiety for Georg and Frieda in their letters) and he left school and started work at a sawmill near Lincoln. Luckily for him, the vicar with whom he was lodging – a man called Walter Freer – was the chess partner of John Spedon Lewish, the founder of the John Lewis department stores. Walter Freer secured a job for Wolfgang at the London store and his success there hinted at his achievements in business later on.

Eva-Maria stayed behind and lived for a while in Göttingen with her prosperous great-uncle Alfred Cöhn. She

---

* This was an institution, founded by Dr Hilde Lion in 1934, which took in German refugees on a charitable basis.

returned to Düsseldorf when he died in March 1938. Alfred (whose lively letters are included here) bequeathed his house to Frieda, but this was appropriated by the Nazis under Forced Purchase Laws (*Zwangsverkauf*). After the war Eva-Maria attempted to reclaim the house as her rightful inheritance, only to be frustrated by bureaucracy.

In November 1938, the assassination of a German diplomat by a Polish Jew led to the infamous *Kristallnacht*. This involved attacks on individual Jews, synagogues and all things Jewish. The events of *Kristallnacht* had a profound effect on the Jewish community in Germany. While there is scarcely any reference to this terrifying experience in the letters (just a brief 'We're quite well'), we know that Georg, Frieda and Eva-Maria were hidden by their friends the Hamachers, having been forewarned of the danger. My mother would describe to me the destruction she witnessed when walking about Düsseldorf on the day after the pogrom, including the remnants of a grand piano that had been ejected from the second-floor window of the apartment belonging to their friends the Mendel family.

Kristallnacht was a turning point. Eva-Maria, who had always been reluctant to leave her parents, finally left Germany in April 1939, at the age of twenty-two. A teacher at Edith's school had organised an entry permit and she lived with a Christian family called Perry in London. Eva-Maria believed that her parents were going to follow her to the Perrys, but this proved not to be the case.

The war years

Once the war began, the letters inevitably became less frequent. Communication was restricted to Red Cross messages, and letters sent undercover by friends in Switzerland and Holland, until their invasion in 1940. The three children were dispersed across England, unable to receive much news of their parents and, at times, of each other.

In 1940 Eva-Maria was interned on the Isle of Man, having been classified as an enemy alien. She became representative of the internees and went on to campaign successfully for better conditions. Eva-Maria was released in 1941 and worked as a secretary at the War Agricultural Executive Committee, living with a reverend in Northallerton.

Meanwhile Edith was not considered an enemy alien as she had been in England since 1937. She started a two-year training course in domestic science and housekeeping at St Mary's Home for Disabled Children in Horam, Sussex, and went on to work as a teacher in various schools.

Wolfgang, like Eva-Maria, had been classified as an enemy alien. He was sent to Australia on the notorious *Dunera*. The journey became infamous for the appalling conditions on board, and the fact that the ship's passengers were a combination of Jewish refugees and German prisoners of war! Wolfgang returned from Australia in December 1941 to join the British Army. He entered Germany on D-Day plus 1 with the 8th King's Royal Irish Hussars tank regiment, ending up in the victory parade in Berlin. He stayed on there until December 1946, acting as an interpreter for the Australian military mission.

Though Georg and Frieda tried frantically to arrange an exit from Germany, in particular by trying to find work in the film industry, this proved impossible. Düsseldorf became a dangerous city for Jews after the war began, and life for Georg and Frieda deteriorated drastically from then on. Both were afflicted by ill health, with Georg undergoing extensive treatment on his teeth, and Frieda suffering from stress. Like all Jews, they were forced to wear the Star of David, and were virtually without any source of income other than the help they received from friends and the little money that came in from the sale of Alfred Cöhn's house in Göttingen. Dr Werner Karthaus, a friend of the family, told my mother after the war that he saw Georg working as a gravedigger in a cemetery, an occupation that must have been totally demoralising for him. Frieda even contemplated suicide, though Georg and some of their friends managed to dissuade her.

Only recently, Wolfgang found a postcard from the USA implying that the application for a visa for Georg and Frieda to emigrate was not far away. Unfortunately that brief window of hope remained closed to them. Georg and Frieda were deported to Minsk on 9 November 1941. Approximately 35,000 people were murdered there, most of them German Jews. Georg and Frieda Lindemeyer were most likely among this number but there is no record of their death.

After the war

The Lindemeyer siblings never returned to Germany to live, but they made frequent visits to address questions of war reparation and to see old friends.

Many of these friends were heroes in their own right, such as Ilse Peters, who is mentioned often in the letters. It was Ilse who enabled the letters to get to and fro, who convinced Frieda not to commit suicide and protected Georg's manuscripts from the Nazis after the deportation to Minsk. I met Ilse Peters when I was a child, and though then too young to understand her true role in the history of my family I do recall the warmth, respect and gratitude my mother showed to her. Indeed this encounter with Ilse Peters is my earliest recollection of the presence of a family tragedy in our history. I was only five years old, but such encounters left a profound, if imprecise, impression on me.

Eva-Maria, Edith and Wolfgang all settled in Britain after the war. Their affiliation to the Jewish and Christian faiths remained ambivalent, but of no practical consequence to how they lived in multiracial, multi-denominational Britain. Wolfgang and Edith both married people from a similar German Jewish background to their own; Wolfgang married Erna Abraham, and Edith married Hans Hirschberg. Neither couple had children. Wolfgang became a very successful businessman, while Edith worked as a teacher. Eva-Maria married my father, Sidney Gilbert, and had three children: my sister Carolyn, my brother Simon and myself.

Edith died in 1996, while Eva-Maria died in March 2005. So only Wolfgang now survives among the siblings.

The letters

As you read these letters, you feel the growing anxiety of the parents for their children, young and far away, but also their belief that their Christian faith would always protect them. But the reason why the letters are so powerful and poignant is because my grandparents' vulnerability is just as apparent as their strength and faith.

As the world became ever more challenging, Georg retreated into the world of his beloved books. He put all his energies into his writing and in his final years was determined to see his work published. In fact his last will and testament stated that it was the 'holy duty' of his children to get his manuscripts published.* Perhaps it was this dream that kept him going. Although his attachment to his three children and wife are evident in his letters, he is clearly at his most animated when discussing books and his own work. He writes to Eva-Maria in 1941.

> . . . of course I am particularly proud that you are attending talks on historical topics – you are your father's daughter after all! Whether it's possible now or only after your release, please make sure that you get

---

* Their father's last request must have weighed heavily on the shoulders of the children. How could they set about getting obscure manuscripts published when their content was of no commercial value? Christoph Moss and the Heinrich Heine institute in Düsseldorf offered to add Georg's surviving works, together with the letters, to their cultural archive. So although still not strictly speaking published, his works will be available to students and academics for posterity. In that sense Georg's wish was fulfilled.

to read Trevelyan's History of England. It's a complete masterpiece, and I'm quite sure there will by now be a second edition of the German translation. And you're even learning to play the violin! Even if you are only able to learn the rudiments in your current circumstances, at least you have taken the first step, and I'm sure that means you'll pick it up again later on.

It did me such a lot of good to read that you have been so responsive to my work. I'm still working on the same thing as when you left. I am actually now getting to the end of it, but it will still take me a considerable time. A while ago I also finished a substantial new legal treatise, and this too has been accepted for publication by 'Geistiges Eigentum', even though its scope goes far beyond the framework of the journal. It is still unclear when or whether the next issue of the journal is due to appear . . .

The world of ideas was always more real to Georg, no doubt his strategy for surviving the terrible final years in Düsseldorf. Both Wolfgang and my mother described him as having his head in the clouds. His friend Werner Karthaus wrote of him as 'a great idealist whose interests were in fact purely intellectual, and who in his artistic endeavors could not easily find his match'. And this is the man we see in the letters.

It is Frieda who grounded him. In these letters, she appears as a woman utterly devoted to her husband and children. Her anxiety about her children is unceasing, even obsessive, though understandably so. But it is this concern that holds the family together and gives the letters so much of their emotional power. She writes to Edith in August 1937:

My dearest Edith,

Now we're missing you dreadfully, but we think about you so much and talk about you constantly, so really you're with us all the time. I'm just looking forward to Christmas, and I hope so much that I'll have my trio together again then. In the end Inter-Aid bought Wolfgang a return ticket [. . .]. Isn't that fabulous? He left Brackley at twenty to eight in the evening and a woman from Inter-Aid met him at Marylebone Station in London. Then he was taken on a tour through London with two other German boys, and they sat and drank coffee before being put onto the train at eleven. He got here at midday and slept seventeen hours straight after I'd bundled him into bed quite against his will. Now he's enjoying his golden freedom, and he's so happy and jolly, just like in the old days . . . have you remembered Uncle Alfred's birthday on 2 August? On 8 August it will have been a year since Aunt Martha died. I hope you've thought of writing to him – he's so generous towards you all, and he always involves himself in your lives.

A thousand kisses,
Mama

Frieda is a mother desperate to have her family under one roof again and utterly helpless to fulfil this wish. I was told Frieda would often go to see the gypsies to have her fortune told, an indication of the helplessness she must have felt. She also suffered very badly from stress all through these years. And yet, for all her helplessness and anxiety, Frieda has a core of strength and courage. She is the communicator in these letters, the organiser and the facilitator (very much in evidence in the letter above), and it is she who manages to keep the family as united as possible. What makes the final letters so terribly moving is that we know her dearest wish – to be together with her family – was never granted. While the earlier letters look forward to future meetings with the children, which to a limited extent do take place, the last letters, simply, but with an infinite sad beauty, see her silently give up hope.

Another remarkable aspect of the letters is that throughout them you are aware there is a kind of illusion occurring in relation to the real-life events. Nowhere is this more obvious than in the letter following the pogrom of Kristallnacht (on 15 November 1938), where there is virtually no reference to the horrors of that day.

In fact the truth of their lives was much worse than the picture the letters painted, and the letters at the end, written by friends of the Lindemeyers to the children after the war, tell a sadder story. But what else could Frieda and Georg communicate other than a bland 'everything is all right', which, inconceivable though it may have been, was the only reassuring message they could send to their children.

The letter written by Frieda to Edith on 21 June 1939 is particularly revealing, and contains a phrase used as the title of the German edition of this book: 'we are only thinking of you'.

21 June 1939
Düsseldorf

FRIEDA TO EDITH

You say that we write so little about ourselves in our letters: well, my child, we are only thinking of you, and so little has happened in my own life since you've all been gone that it simply wouldn't be worth writing about. I go out only rarely. What I like to do most is sit in my little corner and sew or knit, or occupy myself some other way, or listen to the radio. I'm always rather glad when nothing really happens, because news is generally not good news. My only bit of diversion comes with the postman, and my only joy is when he brings a letter from one of you [. . .]

A big fat kiss from Mama [. . .]

And for me that expression, 'we are only thinking of you' sums up the tragedy of my grandparents Georg and Frieda, whom I never met face to face, but now know more about than many close friends, through the extraordinary beauty, sadness and affections of their letters.

David Gilbert
May 2005

Letters

Wolfgang, Edith and Eva-Maria, 1926

1937

Edith Lindemeyer, Georg and Frieda's second child, emigrated to England in February 1937, at the age of seventeen. These letters begin as she takes up a place at Stoatley Rough School in Haslemere, Surrey. Founded by another German emigrant, Dr Hilde Lion, Stoatley Rough was a mixed boarding school intended mainly for refugee children from Nazi Europe.

18 February 1937
Düsseldorf

PARENTS AND EVA-MARIA TO EDITH

My dear girl,

I'm sure you're amazed to have got post from me so soon, but please don't think I'm going to keep spoiling you like this by writing so often. As you can imagine I have a few other things to do. But today I have something in particular to write to you about: the morning after your departure we got a letter addressed to Fräulein Peters saying that the Inter-Aid Committee* had accepted Wolf-

---

* Children's Inter-Aid Committee, founded in March 1936 by agreement between the Central British Fund, Save the Children Fund and the Society *cont'd over/*

gang. He's to travel over after Easter, probably to start at a school in Somerset. You know how very much I'd love to think that you two at least would be together, and Wolfgang, who is rather unhappy at the thought of going to a completely unknown school, would much rather go to Stoatley Rough. Just after you were accepted at Stoatley Rough, Fräulein Peters wrote to ask whether it would be possible for him to go there too, perhaps by doing some kind of swap. To date we haven't had a response. Apparently the letters there are written by different people, and one might not know what the other has written. I thought it might be an idea if you spoke to Fräulein Dr Lion and Dr Wolf as soon as possible. Maybe they could do something to help from that end, but only if they're still prepared to accept Wolfgang, and if the Inter-Aid Committee is prepared to place him there. Please discuss all this with the two ladies as soon as you can and let us know. This is all getting rather urgent, as it's now not very long until Easter. I'd be *so* happy if it worked out! Is Somerset far from where you are? Fräulein Grete's card arrived this morning, which you'd signed. I hope we'll soon hear more about how your trip was, and whether you've made some friends. Do you think you'll be able to settle in well? You know that I want you to tell me *everything*: how you spend your day, what you're reading, if anything at

---

cont'd   of Friends with the special object of looking after Christian children of Jewish extraction. The Inter-Aid Committee sought out children whose anti-Nazi parents had been arrested or were in danger of incarceration. In 1939 this committee joined with the Movement for the Care of Children from Germany to form the Refugee Children's Movement (RCM), chaired by Lord Gorell.

all, and much more besides. Now, my dear child, I hope
with all my heart to have happy news of you soon! Give my
regards to the two ladies.

A thousand loving kisses,
Mama

My dear little miss,

We've been thinking about you all day. I'm trying to
form a picture of the landscape and surroundings of where
you now live – it's not an easy thing to do. We were
delighted to hear that you'd arrived safely. I enclose two
reply coupons.

Many loving kisses,
Papa

PS Give our regards to Hermann!

Dear little thing,

What do you think of your brother now, then!? – In
your next letter *please* send us a postcard with a good
picture of the place. But the letter mustn't be too short. –
How are you getting on with the English? Have you
spoken much yet? Tomorrow morning I'm really going
to start working on Wolfgang's English with him. That's
all for today.

1000000 kisses,
Eva-Maria

24 February 1937
Düsseldorf

PARENTS AND EVA-MARIA TO EDITH

My dear child,

We were so glad to have your first letter and hope with all our hearts that you're now even more settled and already quite happy to be there. It's just wonderful that you have your own room, and with a proper light, too! But please don't abuse this privilege by reading or writing at night. Sleep is more important than anything else!!! If you don't get the time to write during the day, I'd much rather wait longer for your letters. You *must* have your rest. Your evening walk to your lodgings will, I'm sure, be very good for you. But, please, always carry a loud whistle. You'd feel much safer if you had one, because if need be you could always make yourself heard. If you can't get hold of a whistle there, I'll gladly send you one. And how is your English? Can you already make yourself understood? Yesterday Wolfgang had his first English lesson with a retired teacher from the Luisenschule, an aunt of Frau Grüters. Hopefully he'll make quick progress. It's now been confirmed that just after Easter he'll be starting at the school in Bath, near Bristol. I still don't know if that's far away from you, but I hope to find out soon. I don't know what kind of school it is either, and I'd so like to know more. I would love to bring him there myself (even though I'm terrified of getting seasick), but I'm not yet sure whether that will be possible. Uncle Alfred thinks it would be much better if I went over to visit you both a bit later. Maybe I'll be able to persuade him that I'd find it much easier to be separated from you if I could picture where you're both living. I'm so looking forward to seeing it. I hope you and Hermann have now got over your seasickness, and that you're both healthy and jolly.

Frau Herz is quite upset that she still doesn't know whether or not Lore has been accepted at Stoatley Rough for the autumn. She's going to start looking around for something else. We both think it's such a shame, as we'd have loved you to be there together. Could you mention once again that Frau Herz hasn't yet had a response to either of her letters? Now to something else: what did you do with the rest of the material you used to make your duvet cover? I need it urgently for Wolfgang. If I come to England, I *might* even come and visit you!!! But I don't know what I'll do about staying overnight, with so little money, and Wolfgang wants to come and see you too before I bring him to Bath. I asked Fräulein Grete whether she might be able to find a cheap room for us both, so I've just got to wait and see how or whether it will all work out. If you have the time, please write as extensively as possible about what you're up to!

A thousand warm kisses,

Mama

Dear Edith,

We were so delighted by your letter. I hope it really is the case that you're well. Mama will send money in the next few

days, and Eva-Maria's will follow. Yesterday she applied
for the relevant permit.*

Warmest wishes,
Papa

My dear thing,

The old folk always leave me so little space to write, but I
promise to send you a long letter very soon. You know that
if there's something private you want to say to me, you can
always write to Ruth! Then you could be honest about how
it really is. Do you already speak perfect English? I can just
imagine you chatting away to all those English people! On
Saturday I'm going to the zoo with Jansenwirth again, but
this time I'll behave better. Is the food any good over there?

A thousand kisses from Eva-Maria

7 March 1937
Düsseldorf

PARENTS TO EDITH

My dear child,

Your last letter did at least give us a better picture of your
life over there. You know we're interested in everything,
and how we'd like to know about all the things you're
doing, but your letters simply *must* be neater. The way you
so carelessly rip the sheets of paper off the pad so that they

---

* Here and in subsequent letters this probably refers to a permit which regulated
the amount of money an individual was allowed to send abroad. At this time the
limit was 10 Marks per month.

tear makes me wonder whether your letters to us are equally uncaring. And I'm sure that's not your intention. So then, next time you'll tear the sheets off more gently, won't you?!

Yesterday, in the same post as your letter, there was one from Grete asking for your address. Please get in touch with her soon. It was really kind of her to collect you so late at night in London and help you on your way. I asked her how much a room would cost in London. In the meantime I've discovered here that you'd have to pay six shillings per person per night. If that's the case we wouldn't get very far with our grand fortune of ten Marks. If we could stay with your landlady for one shilling and sixpence per night, that would be amazingly cheap. I'd like to have the opportunity to see something of London but, well, we'll see what happens.

For a whole week we have had no further news about Wolfgang's prospects. I'll write as soon as I know any more. – Tomorrow I'll send a small packet off to you, and hope that you find its contents taste delicious. Did you get the registered letter with the money? Please always tell me what you've had from us so we know that everything has arrived safely. As soon as Eva-Maria's permit gets here (she applied for it a week ago), I'll send you her ten Marks, and I'll send you mine for the month the moment I know when I'll be travelling.

I'm particularly glad you're getting on well with one of the girls, and I hope that friendship continues. It surprised me to hear that the Jewish spirit is so dominant there. Are Fräulein Dr Lion and Dr Wolf both Jewish? I thought they were Protestant non-Aryans. How many Christian children have you got there? You should seriously consider whether it is actually right to try to influence the children. Of course, I can't judge from here, but I just wanted you to think about it. – I find it hilarious that you're giving German lessons. Why not give spelling lessons too??!! Judging by your work schedule, you must be an extremely busy person. How are your English lessons going? Wolfgang is very enthusiastic about his English and has two lessons a week. He's making very good progress.

You ask how our work is going. Well, it's the same as ever really. By the way, Dr Feldner wrote from Hamburg to say that the job in question had been filled through a restructuring of the administrative division. They said they'd bear Papa in mind, and perhaps recommend him elsewhere. I doubt anything will come of it, but we'll wait and see.

The blue material for the duvet cover doesn't seem to be in the white cupboard. Could you think where else you might have put it, and let me know soon!

A thousand kisses from your Mama

PS If you've got time, do write to Fräulein Poensgen and Uncle Alfred, but please make sure you write clearly and cleanly!!! Uncle Alfred sent the enclosed reply coupons for you.

Dearest Mouse,

Many thanks for your letter! As you go about your religious activities, please always remember that tolerance is the highest precept of any world view or religion, and that

Judaism is Christianity's elder brother. Yesterday I gave my Grabbe talk in Elberfeld, and it went down extremely well. Frau Barmé in particular thanked me repeatedly, and was quite emotional! I've also been asked to give my talk on Schiller, Kleist and Hebbel sometime.

Warm wishes and many kisses,

Papa

14 March 1937
Düsseldorf

GEORG AND EVA-MARIA TO EDITH

Dear Edith,

We were so thrilled with your letter, in which you made your points with such deep sensitivity and a clear eye for the actual circumstances. You probably found a great deal there that was quite different from what you had expected, and I'm sure you have some difficult tasks to tackle. It may not be at all obvious how and when things will get any easier, but there is no other road than the one which you are now travelling, and it's quite possible that this demanding school is the best one that there is for you. It has to be the case that by overcoming these problems you will not only free your path of obstacles, but also become more mature in the process.

The split of the Paulusbund is not such a terrible thing. I'm sure Mama will write at greater length about it. I hope that our branch of it will be able to stick together in some form, and perhaps even continue with our intellectual efforts. I'm delighted that you enjoyed 'Avalun'. If anyone else at your school is interested in the book, I could of course send a few more copies over, one in every parcel for example; I've still got a small supply here. If they want to (and can) pay for it, you could work it out at one and a half or two shillings per copy, and of course keep the money for yourself.

I'm so very much looking forward to the letter you say is on its way. In the meantime stay well and keep your chin up!

Heartfelt kisses (as many as you like),

Papa

Dear Edith,

Your letter arrived this morning – we had all been so looking forward to it. But now Mama always expects your letters on Saturday afternoons. Can't you send them off like you did before, so that they arrive on Saturday? Mama enjoys Sundays so much more when she's already had your letter the day before. Please write and tell us how your English is. Can you have a conversation and make yourself understood, or do you still find that quite hard? My Spanish is now going quite well, and you can imagine how pleased I am about that. I'm also teaching myself English shorthand and – much to Papa's horror – learning the piano from scratch again so that I might even be able to play something before long. Unfortunately I don't really have enough time to practise. Today I was supposed to go and visit Grandma in Elberfeld, but it's pouring with rain so I'm not allowed. The other day I went with Papa to see *Carmen* at the

'Halunkenloge'. It was quite brilliant. Wolfgang can't add a note here because he's at the Hamachers'. Ruth sends regards too.

>10000000 kisses, my dear snotbag,
>from your Eva-Maria

17 March 1937
Göttingen

ALFRED CÖHN TO EDITH

Dear Edith

I was so glad to get your letter, and also news of you via your mother. You clever, brave creature, you really are getting to grips with your new life. It already seems to be clear to you that the good things to be had there have to be courted, as at the same time you have so many duties which are rather more strenuous than pleasurable. With any luck, when they recognise your positive attitude and what you have achieved, they will allow you to do you more varied tasks, and what you learn from them will stand you in good stead for life. Above all I hope you're being forced to speak a great deal of English, so that it will soon become quite effortless. When you are in another country, you should learn its language like a child learns the mother tongue, i.e. without grammar. I'm sure you're aware that I'm opposed to all learning, or at least to unnecessary learning. I think of myself as someone who speaks and writes reasonably good German, but I know very little indeed about German grammar. And I'm going to let you into a little secret which is very useful when you're learning a foreign language: courage is an extremely good substitute for grammar!

And now to something much more important than grammar. I hear that I am allowed to send parcels over to England full of all kinds of wonderful things. So do me the pleasure and send a note to say what you'd most like. Otherwise I'd end up sending chocolate only to find you don't like it, or a book you've already got. If there's the odd little request, please send it to me and not home, and I'll see what I can do.

I can well imagine that you don't have much time to write, and I'm sure there are many people who'd like to receive letters from you, but I also hope that it will be my turn once in a while. I'd always be delighted to hear how everything is with you.

Warm wishes,
Uncle Alfred

5 April 1937
Düsseldorf

PARENTS TO EDITH
My dear child,

Despite my good intentions, I didn't write my usual Sunday letter to you. I had such terrible neuralgia that I simply couldn't. Today I'm feeling much better so I'm getting through my chores as quickly as I can. In fact yesterday wasn't really a proper Sunday for me at all because your letter had already arrived on Friday. By Sunday I'd read it for the umpteenth time, but I still didn't manage to sit down and write to you. It gives me more and more pleasure to get your letters. Very gradually I'm getting to know Stoatley Rough through them, and I've actually got quite a clear picture of much of the school. Don't lose sleep over the fact that you can't speak enough English yet. It will all suddenly fall into place!

This morning I met up with Anneli Köhrmann (who, by the way, looked quite delightful). She spent a time working in a household in England and explained to me that she could neither understand nor speak English for at least half a year. Just as she was about to give up hope of ever learning it, all of a sudden she could do it, just like that. So take in everything that's said to you, learn what you can, and during this hopefully carefree period build your resources to cope with life later on. That's the best that I could wish for you from your time over there! And as soon as you've been there long enough to acquire some basic skills, keep your eyes open for a trainee post. Please try to discuss your progress with Dr Lion and Dr Wolf at every stage. I'm convinced that they would be able to judge everything much better than we can from here. And whatever happens don't think that you have to earn money immediately! That's really not the most important thing. Above all you have to develop into a healthy, sensible human being who can step out in life when the time comes with a sizeable appetite for living, a great deal of energy and a fair amount of diligence. For you that time has not yet come, so just enjoy yourself with the others!

Did you get the Easter eggs? I packed them up with so much love that I would be mortified if they hadn't arrived safely. Next Sunday you'll probably be in London! I hope you have lovely weather and lots of fun!

Now, my treasure, farewell and many loving kisses,

Mama

Dear child,

Today I've got some news for you which isn't altogether unfavourable. The lawyer Levy-Ries used to represent Wilhelm Saatz (the coal company), but now that he has moved to London this contract has been passed on to me, and I'm to get a 5% commission. I've already attracted a whole lot of clients who have promised me contracts. Otherwise there's no news.

Kisses from Papa

11 April 1937
Düsseldorf

FRIEDA TO EDITH

My dear girl,

You'll be in London now, and I hope you have a wonderful day there and get to see lots of things. I know from experience that your work will seem all the sweeter after a day like that. Now I have to ask you to answer *all* the questions I put in my letters. For example, I asked whether the housekeeping pupils all had the same amount of work, or do you have more than most? Then I wanted to know whether you speak German or English among yourselves, and whether the cookery classes and other lessons are conducted in German or English, and then I asked how the food is. What do you get for lunch and dinner? Are you able to slip Hermann Grünebaum an extra slice of bread and butter, as his mother would wish? – I was so glad to read that you now have a little more confidence in your future ability in English. Just speak as much as you can and read as much as possible, and then it will come. It's wonderful that you're teaching German, and it would be even better if you remembered for example that *nämlich* is spelled without *h*, and *hässlich* with *ch* and not *g*. You know very well that your German spelling is wobbly, so you'll have to be extra careful that you don't teach some poor child something that's wrong. That could be really embarrassing.

You ask how my health is: well, these neuralgias torment me a great deal, but I can cope with them. Papa helps me out a lot and a few days ago the two of us cleaned the entire apartment together. Frau Hohaus comes twice a week (when she's not ill, that is). But she's just not a well person, and I can't rely on her, despite her good intentions.

This morning I left church with Fräulein Jung and we walked through the Hofgarten. She sends her very best regards, as do a whole lot of other people. Everyone's always asking me to pass on their good wishes, but I often forget. Just now I can only remember Fräulein Peters and the Kaumanns. Uncle Alfred writes us the sweetest letters. It's amazing that his work has appeared in the Goethe yearbooks. He's always delighted to receive the letters that I pass on, so sometime it would be a good idea if you enclosed an extra note especially for him. He doesn't have a great deal of joy in his life, but you know he adores you and

Eva-Maria, and he acknowledges this by helping out where
he can. For that we owe him a great deal of thanks.

A thousand and one big kisses, my dear child,

from Mama

PS Wolfgang is quite put out that you haven't yet sent him a
card.

18 April 1937
Düsseldorf

PARENTS AND EVA-MARIA TO EDITH

Dear Mouse,

Many thanks for your lovely letter! So it appears that
'King Oedipus' didn't impress you, which for Sophocles'
sake I deeply regret. I'm glad you're getting on well with
Hermann. I think Wolfgang will also begin to thrive when
he's over there. Soon you'll be together with him and
Mama, which makes me very happy for you all. It'll
probably be summer before you and I see each other again,
but that's not so far off now.

Many loving kisses,

Papa

Dear Snotbag,

Thank you for your dear letter. I can well imagine what a
wonderful time you had in London. I'd so like to visit
London sometime myself. I'm sure Berlin is like a small
town in comparison, isn't it? Fräulein Grete and Ellen will
doubtless lead a fine life there. – You'll be seeing Mama and

Wolfgang soon, and then it won't be such a long time until the holidays!

I'm still working hard at my English shorthand; Ruth [Schoen] and I practise it together. On Tuesday they're putting on 'Faust Part 1' here. We so wanted to go and see it, but the seats are ridiculously expensive. On Friday, Papa, Mama, Wolfgang and I went to the Alhambra to see 'Etappenhasen' and we laughed our heads off. I don't think we've all laughed so much at the same time ever. On Tuesday we're moving the office into the apartment – you can imagine how thrilled I am at the prospect.* The worst thing of all is that the Evil One left yesterday to start another job next week. We've already found a new girl but she only comes next Wednesday, after we've already moved everything. Apparently she's only sixteen.

100000000 kisses,
Eva-Maria

25 April 1937
Düsseldorf

FRIEDA TO EDITH

My dearest, most lovely Birthday Girl,

All my thoughts will be with you on the day, so I'll be completely distracted from all the things I've got to get done here. It's the very first time that one of my children has begun a new year of their life away from me. What a strange feeling! – I feel like I've suddenly aged. I'll be thinking about

---

* Georg Lindemeyer's office where he practised as a lawyer.

your future even more than usual, and for you, for all of us, my wishes are even warmer, even more from the heart. The best and most wonderful thing I can hope for you, my dear child, is that this year enables you to step out in the right direction towards the fulfilment of your ambitions in life, and that you are able to see clearly where this path is taking you, and what you have to do to make progress along it. From this distance it's terribly difficult to comment on all your plans: we don't know the circumstances over there, and you yourself don't yet seem to have anything tangible to aim for. I'm just glad that we will soon have the opportunity to talk face to face about all the issues that concern us most. – I think it's excellent that you're now sharing a bedroom with an English girl. Then you'll certainly have to speak more, and that can only be good for your knowledge of the language.

Now I want to explain the latest with Wolfgang: it's been decided once and for all that he'll be going to Magdalen College in Brackley, and not to Bath. Brackley is 75 km away from London, somewhere near Oxford. I don't know any more, and each day I wait for news as to when he's supposed to start there. I don't think you need to book a driver for us. We can save ourselves the two shillings and sixpence by walking up together, and we've all got such a huge amount to catch up on. I still have no idea whether it's best to go via Vlissingen or Ostend.

Tomorrow evening at ten o'clock, the day before your birthday, I'll say out loud 'My dear child, sleep well into the next year of your life', and at that moment you must think of me as hard as you can. It'll be as though I'm talking to you at your bedside after you've said your prayers. Shall we do it like that!? So, my love, look forward to the time when we'll be together again, and remember that all this will pass!

Countless kisses and hugs, my Birthday Girl,

from your Mama

27 April 1937
Düsseldorf

FRIEDA TO EDITH

My dear child,

Today it's your birthday! We'll be thinking of you all day long, and I hope you'll be able to feel that. We'll be coming over on Friday 7 May and want to stay with you until the Monday morning. Could you let me know as soon as possible if you can get hold of the following for Wolfgang: two bottom sheets, two top sheets, three pillows, three pairs of white socks, three sports shirts and three pairs of shorts. And do say if you want us to bring you anything from here.

I enclose a letter for Fräulein Dr Lion, warning her of our visit to Haslemere! I think it's only good manners to ask her permission. I've also written to Fräulein Grete. Wolfgang has to register at Woburn House when we get to London. How do I get to Waterloo Station? We're probably going to go via Vlissingen now. So, my dear girl, we'll be seeing each other soon.

A thousand kisses,

Mama

Frieda and Wolfgang travelled to England in early May 1937, spending the weekend at Stoatley Rough with Edith before going on to London. Frieda said goodbye to her son at the Inter-Aid Committee offices, from where he was accompanied to his new school, Magdalen College in Brackley, Northamptonshire. Frieda and Edith had arranged to meet up once more in London before Frieda's return to Germany, but preparations for the coronation of George VI on 12 May 1937 prevented them from doing so.

11 May 1937
London

FRIEDA TO EDITH

My dear Edith,

I find it so hard that I couldn't give us both the pleasure of having you come up to London. You can't imagine what it looks like here. There are barriers everywhere, and you simply can't get through them. We wouldn't even have been able to meet up; it's impossible to get from Alexandra Road, where I am, to Waterloo. It would have been such a dreadful shame if you'd spent all that money only to end up sitting there at Waterloo Station, with me stuck here. It would have been nice to talk with you again. Today really sapped me of all my strength. The poor boy really struggled to be brave, but even so it nearly broke our hearts. I'll stop off somewhere on the way home to try and pull myself together to cope with this life. Whether and how I'll manage it I just don't know.

The people at Inter-Aid were very friendly. Mrs Schwab

said she'd get in touch with Fräulein Dr Lion about training possibilities for you and give advice about what you should be doing. The main thing is that they're keen to help. I've just heard that I can't travel tomorrow because the Underground trains aren't running, so I'll be sitting here all on my own, feeling so sad. It would have been so lovely if we'd had a few more hours together, but it's not to be. I hope with all my heart that you'll follow my good advice and do your best to accept everything uncritically, without taking offence. Don't always think about how things could be different. Try and copy what the others do. You have inherited some of my willpower, so I'm sure you'll succeed!

A thousand warm, sweet kisses, my dear child,

from your Mama

16 May 1937
Düsseldorf

PARENTS TO EDITH

My dear child,

To save on postage, I'm enclosing this letter with one I'm sending to Fräulein Dr Lion. Of course I'm sad that we couldn't see each other one more time, but, please believe me, it would have been a complete impossibility to meet up at a certain place at a certain time, especially when neither of us knows our way around. I couldn't have exposed you to the possible dangers of undertaking such a journey that day. We should be grateful that we were able to meet up and recognise once again just how much we love each other, and that no separation by land or sea can part us or

distance us from each other in our hearts. I am so happy
that you can make me a part of your life through your
letters, and share what you are experiencing both emotionally and otherwise. Now I can visualise you lying in
bed at night, and I accompany you through each hour of
your day. The landscape is so indescribably beautiful – it
must be a great joy just to be there. I am quite convinced
that things would pick up if you would begin to accept
everything that's demanded of you as it is, and not as you
think it should or could be. Believe me, there is something
positive in absolutely everything even if it's different from
how you might have imagined it. If only for my sake please
try to do the purely technical things as you are being asked
to, and accept each person around you for what they are,
not as you would wish them to be. Even if at first you have
to force yourself to do all this consciously, because I'm
asking you to, you'll learn through experience that this is
the only way you can get through life; the world can never
be fashioned into what you want it to be. Instead you have
to grin and bear it; you have to face everything life throws
at you with composure, not display hostility. If you try to
battle against all adversities, not only personally but also in
your environment, the impossibility of success will only
demoralise you.

We still haven't heard from Wolfgang, although yesterday Herbert Hamacher got a very sweet card from him for
his birthday. Today the headmaster wrote to say that he
seemed to have settled in well during the holidays, and that
he hoped that Wolfgang might be able to follow the lessons
a little in a week or two.

Next week I'll write more – there's still so much to say. That's all for today.

Warm kisses, my girl, from your Mama

PS I should tell you that this is the first letter I'm writing in my new writing case. I'm so delighted with it.

Dear Mouse,

Since I've been forbidden to start a new sheet of paper – for fear of the letter getting too heavy – I'm going to have to be brief. How are you getting on with the Oedipus book? Which translation do you need? I don't have a spare copy of 'King Oedipus', but I could get you another quite cheaply.

Many kisses,

Papa

30 May 1937
Göttingen

ALFRED CÖHN TO EDITH

Dear Edith,

Today's wonderful news is that Eva-Maria arrived last night and will be here for three whole weeks. She's beginning her stay by learning how to become an early riser. You see, it's only ten in the morning and when I knocked just now she said she was getting up! Your mother has told me what's going on in your life. Everything sounds marvellous, but I was most disappointed to hear that you're no longer doing handicraft lessons. They would have been so useful to you in all kinds of ways.

By the way, Frau Professor Bousset, whom you met once at my place, speaks of your two ladies, Dr Lion and Dr Wolf, with the greatest respect. She believes one of them has given talks here in Göttingen. If you thought it appropriate to give them, or at least one of them, my Pandora essay, I'd very gladly send you another copy.

Now I'm going to have to give you a bit of a ticking-off: you were supposed to be writing to tell me what you wanted in your next parcel, but here I'm sitting again, unable to think of anything other than silly sweets. Eva-Maria is going out tomorrow to look for things to send you, so I hereby absolve myself of all responsibility.

> All best wishes from Uncle Alfred

> *30 May 1937*
> *Düsseldorf*

FRIEDA TO EDITH

My dear child,

Today is Sunday, and we're sitting here all alone thinking about you three. Eva-Maria went to Göttingen yesterday for three weeks, and I hope she'll be able to have a good rest there. Typical that your letter didn't get here today, of all days. There must have been some postal delay. But I'm writing to you now anyway because tomorrow I may not have the time. I won't post this until yours has arrived, just in case you've got any questions that need to be answered.

Now I have a few urgent questions for you: yesterday Frau Grünebaum told me that she'd received a letter with the new school dates (I've not yet got a copy), and apparently we should be letting them know by 31 May who is coming home for the holidays on 15 July. Despite all my best efforts, I've still not managed to send you the money or the ticket for the trip. Please speak to Dr Lion about this. It would be so lovely if she could see a way of doing it, and you know how delighted we would all be. I'm not convinced it's justifiable for us to spend the 64 Marks for the fare for such a short time, even if we *could* find the money – the holidays only last until 20 August. Wolfgang has holidays from 28 July until 15 September. That's a significantly longer time, but even so we're not at all certain that it will be possible. His headmaster would much rather send him off to a camp with the Scouts. Of course I would find all this hard to bear. Ever since you've all been gone I've lived only for the holidays, but if there really is no way of doing it I'll just have to swallow my disappointment yet again.

Did you get the money on Eva-Maria's permit? This month it will only arrive on the 21st, because that's when she's back. On mine I'll send it off promptly on the first. Could you send some money on to Wolfgang? The poor boy has none. I enclose a copy of his letter, where he says that he can't write to you as he doesn't have enough money for the postage. On the whole his letters are very reassuring – their tone shows that he's not too unhappy there.

How's your sore finger? Give it a kiss from me,

Mama

6 June 1937
Düsseldorf

FRIEDA TO EDITH

My dear, dear girl,

Having read your letter of today, I now know why I've been thinking about you so anxiously this week. I just had the feeling that you needed me. It's so strange to realise at times like this how close and interwoven our lives are, and that despite the many kilometres that separate us we can still sense when there's something wrong. I think we should be very grateful indeed to Dr Lion that she dissuaded you from taking on this job, and for the fact that she wants to help you develop your skills. Someone else in her position might have been only too glad to use the opportunity to get rid of a pupil who doesn't pay, without even having to worry too much about it. You have cause to be extremely thankful to her, and I know my Edith well enough to be satisfied that she will put this sense of gratitude into action by dedicating herself with all her strength to the duties and tasks that have been assigned to her. I think Dr Lion's conduct in this matter was impeccable – please give her the enclosed thank-you note. Listen, it just doesn't make sense for you to take on a job like that just now, without any prospect of learning something from it. It would be quite different if you had a confirmed apprenticeship for the foreseeable future and it were just a question of doing something in the interim, so as not to take advantage of Dr Lion's generosity for too long.

So are you able to stay on at Stoatley Rough for the time being, and learn all those things you so want to know? That would be just lovely – your stay there seems to be suiting you, and to be honest you haven't looked so well in a long time.

Please write in detail about everything you're learning and doing. You wouldn't believe how important to me those days are when I get post, your letters on Sundays and Wolfgang's on Tuesdays. I feel like someone who has been led to a spring and allowed to drink, and once I've written my reply I immediately start imagining what you'll be writing in your next one. When your letter arrives next Sunday I'll be all on my own. Papa has been invited away for a few days – you know, like last year – and Eva-Maria will be in Göttingen for two more weeks.

I've almost finished the spring-cleaning – it was a huge amount of work, but now everything looks wonderful. Now I'm going to try and rent out a room, and I'll look for an afternoon job. As far as the holidays are concerned, you are probably right: first of all, you have to stay there if they need you, because of course they're helping you and you can't just leave them in the lurch, and, secondly, you're right about the money issue. We both know just how painful it will be for me, but we *must* be sensible, no matter how hard that is. Do you think you'll be able to come for Christmas? Do the housekeeping trainees get time off at Christmas? Soon Papa will have to look into the question of when you become an expatriate German, and what the consequences of that will be for you.* I'll set it out for you

---

* Frieda may have been referring to a law implemented by the National Socialists in July 1933 which withdrew German citizenship from Germans living abroad if it was deemed that their behaviour 'damaged Germany's interests'.

in a letter. If Wolfgang came to see us now, we'd almost certainly have to spend Christmas without him. I don't know what I should do, or what's for the best. You didn't need to send Wolfgang as much as ten shillings. It really isn't necessary for him to have so much money; if you send him a shilling or two from time to time, that should be ample. That's all for today. Be brave and be good, my dear child.

A big hug and kisses from your Mama

12 June 1937
Düsseldorf

FRIEDA TO EDITH

My dear, dear girl,

Your lovely letter arrived already today, Saturday, and I'm all alone with you, listening to your news, and even though I've now finished reading the letter I'm still listening to you and chatting with you. And you, my big girl, have been sitting on my lap, talking and talking, and we've been cuddling each other. It was really wonderful. It's such a shame we can't send parcels any more. Please write and let me know the moment it's allowed again, and I'll send you something really delicious.

On Thursday I was invited by Frau Grossmann to Café Kurten for breakfast. It was so plush! She was very sweet, and told me that her children spend the afternoons with Frau Berger, but they're not terribly happy there. I'm so glad you're doing some sewing and other handicrafts, and it's wonderful that you're learning bookkeeping too. Please don't accept a post anywhere else yet, just learn, learn, learn! I told Frau Herz and the others how well Dr Lion acted in that particular matter. Everyone thinks her conduct was very impressive, and it certainly won her a great deal of admiration here. Did you pass on the letter I sent for her the other week?

Sometimes I really don't mind this solitude. I never have to hurry to get things done on time, and I can do as I like, but I'm not somebody who was born to be alone for any length of time. I will only be really happy if I have the full complement of my children gathered round me once again. I would *so* love to have a good photograph of you and Wolfgang! Do you think you would be able to get one done sometime? I'd like that more than anything else in the world. – Another night has now passed and Sunday is here. This afternoon I'm off to the Kaumanns'. Eva-Maria comes home a week today. I just hope she's had a good rest – she certainly desperately needed one. I'll probably go to Göttingen soon too, and if I didn't have so many things to worry I'd certainly look forward to a break. Uncle Alfred sent me ten Marks in order to soothe Eva-Maria's bad conscience at having such a nice time there, so he says. He really is such a wonderful man. The only thing is I wouldn't be able to do that much walking with him; I am always tired, and he's soon to be seventy-four. I would most like to be there for his birthday and for the anniversary of Aunt Martha's death on 6 August, but that won't work out, not with the best will in the world. I find it hard that you won't be here for Papa's fiftieth birthday. Of course I can understand that it's simply impossible, but still, I'm very sad about it.

On Tuesday we received an invitation from Wolfgang's headmaster to a Speech Day at the school on 26 June. I would certainly have gone if there weren't so many obstacles! His wife also wrote a quite charming letter saying that Wolfgang has made good progress and gets on well with the other boys. Apparently he has a wonderful, healthy complexion, and the rather gloomy, tired face he arrived with now has a completely different expression. I was *so* delighted. Everything seems to be going so well. He hasn't yet caught up with the others in French and Maths, but I hope he's now realised that a great deal depends on him studying hard. So, my darling, I'm so looking forward to your next letter and hold you very close to my heart,

Mama

20 June 1937
Düsseldorf

FRIEDA TO EDITH
My dear Edith,

I sent a parcel off to you yesterday afternoon with the coat I promised and a slice of birthday cake, so that on Thursday you can imagine we are together. It's the first cake I've made since you've all been away and, alongside all the good ingredients, I've baked so much love into it. I so wanted to send you all sorts of goodies, but I was too nervous about customs and so on. It would be lovely if you could magic something halfway decent for yourself out of the coat.

Do other children come to stay at Stoatley Rough during the holidays? What do you all get up to otherwise when most of the children are away? I'll certainly get you the book you mentioned while I was there, but I can't quite remember what it was called – I seem to be suffering from memory loss, probably due to premature old age. So please send me the title again, and I'll try to find it for you.

I probably will be going to Göttingen on Friday, but I haven't completely made up my mind yet. I could surely do with a rest, but I wouldn't be very good company for Uncle Alfred. Grandma is here today, Sunday. I asked her to come today rather than on my birthday on Thursday, which is when she planned to. I don't even want to think about that day this year. It was always so wonderful when the three of you were gathered round, you coming out with your little poem, and all of you doing your very best to make it a happy day. Often you were all quite reckless, spending far too much money on me, but it was heavenly to see and feel your love time and time again! I know you are attached to me and always will be, wherever you are in the world, but we creatures appear to be strangely equipped in that we also want to be able to see each other and hold each other tight.

Now, my dear girl, I hope you are thinking of me as much as I am thinking of you!

Infinite loving kisses from Mama

21 June 1937
Göttingen

UNCLE ALFRED TO EDITH

Dear Edith,

Eva-Maria went home yesterday after her three-week stay. Most mornings she went to the open-air swimming pool, and in the afternoons she sunbathed on a deckchair in the garden. I would love to have her to stay permanently, but unfortunately she hasn't been able to find a job here yet.

You must have sent off your letter to me before you received my second, in which I urged you to write down your wishes for your next parcels. I've already heard about the obligatory sweets, and the only other thing you mention is Lou Andreas Salomé's book on Rilke. I have a copy of the book, but I don't want to send it to you. I don't understand why you should think it's of any value at all! According to this book, which by the way is written in particularly difficult German, the *real* Rilke is the man who composed the Duinese Elegies and the Sonnets to Orpheus. If you have read and got to grips with them, then you might be able to explain them to me sometime, because I don't understand them at all. I do think they express some nice ideas, but not one of those poems has made a lasting impression on me. On the whole I find them quite pompous, dense and morbid. They're rather improper, and vague too. All my life I've tried to express myself clearly, vividly and precisely, and I've used Goethe as a model for this. Lou's book (you know, of course, that she is a friend of mine, and I've often discussed Rilke with her) seeks to show you that those bits of Rilke you thought you understood you have in fact fundamentally misconstrued. If you insist upon it, I will of course lend you the book for a while, but I would much rather you read something else.

Eva-Maria read lots of wonderful books while she was here. She particularly enjoyed Dickens' *A Tale of Two Cities*. Wouldn't you be able to read that in English?

23 June – this letter has been sitting around for a couple of days, and as I read through it again, I thought of a nice little experiment we could do. I expect your mother to arrive on Friday, the day after tomorrow, and to stay for two weeks. She is a voracious reader, so I'll give her Lou's book and see what she has to say about it. I won't try to influence her at all – I'll just tell her that you want to read it. I promise to tell you exactly what she says, and I'll do whatever she wants me to do. If you write to me, or to her while she's here, don't forget to send your wish-list, which I'll then be able to discuss with her. I hope she'll have as good a rest as Eva-Maria did.

All good wishes from Uncle Alfred

29 June 1937
Göttingen

FRIEDA TO EDITH (incomplete)
My dear, dear girl,

You gave me so much joy on my birthday! The tablecloth is simply wonderful – I was so proud to lay it out, and I'm delighted by it. I don't think it's too ornate at all! I loved your letter, and particularly your poem. Your account of what I did on the day was almost spot-on, but Eva-Maria couldn't drag me off to the cinema. I simply didn't feel like it

– I missed you all too much. In the evening we read a
Jacobsen novella together, and otherwise I was rather busy
all day, even more than normal as I came to Göttingen the
following day. Unfortunately Frau Hohaus is ill again and
can't help with my deliveries at all, so I did everything for
that period in advance, and Papa will do the other bits and
pieces with one of the Hamachers. It simply has to work out
for the two weeks, and when I'm back everything will be a
little easier.

Shall I tell you what Uncle Alfred said to me? He told me
that I might be able to come over to England again sometime soon!! For the time being I'm only dreaming of it, but
the prospect that it might be possible again makes me very
happy. The few days I spent with you were so lovely . . .

5 July 1937
Göttingen

FRIEDA TO EDITH

My love,

Your dear letter has just arrived. I'm glad its tone is
slightly different from the previous one, but in all your
letters I can read a fair bit between the lines that comes close
to that same tone. You *must not* encumber your progress by
grumbling and being moody – it'll only restrict and paralyse
you. If you stopped asking yourself at every turn how this or
that might benefit you, you would get your work done with
very different results. Of course you should devote the
greatest effort and enthusiasm to those areas which are
most important to you, but don't you think the other things

might also help indirectly? All kinds of skills which might be irrelevant in day-to-day life are essential for craftwork – I'm sure you'll have noticed how the arts and crafts often have quite different influences, and link up with all kinds of subjects that are in fact quite dissimilar. Come on, don't let it get you down!

On Wednesday Uncle Alfred and I sent you some material for a dress and some sewing silk. We chose it together, as a present from him. It's quite lovely, with colourful stripes, and I'm certain you'll like it. Since you didn't mention its arrival in today's letter, we are already beginning to worry that the parcel might have gone astray. We'd both be so upset. Please send a postcard to Uncle Alfred as soon as you get it, and let me know at the same time whether you need anything else for the dress, like a blue belt perhaps, or something for the collar?

Today Papa sent on a letter from the Inter-Aid Committee asking whether I'd rather Wolfgang came home for the summer holidays or at Christmas. I have no idea what I should write in reply. The journey via Southampton is far too expensive for us, and to get to Hamburg alone costs almost as much as the entire fare via Ostend. And then what about Christmas? It would be so lovely if we could all be together for that, and, besides, the boy has his birthday then and I really can't bear to think of him spending those days among strangers! I'll wait until his letter arrives tomorrow, and then perhaps I'll leave it up to him to decide. Please tell Hermann all about everything there, and I'll go to Elberfeld as soon as I can to talk to him myself. My time here is nearly at an end and I feel thoroughly relaxed here – I've spent my days lying out in the garden. – Well now, my dear child, make sure you look after yourself.

Warm kisses from your Mama

PS I'm to send best wishes from Uncle Alfred. You say that you wish you hadn't sent me that last letter, but I completely disagree! If you can't share these things with me, who else do you have to turn to? You must always tell me about what is weighing on your heart, even it's not easy to set down on paper. Please be straight with me, always.

11 July 1937
Düsseldorf

PARENTS TO EDITH

My dear girl,

I'm now at home again and really rather pleased to be here. Such absolute peace and quiet is not quite the right thing for me at the moment, in my present emotional state, and physical relaxation is not appropriate either in the circumstances. But don't write anything about this in your letters – Uncle Alfred only wanted to do what he thought was best.

Imagine this: when I got home late last night, feeling so sad because I remembered how you three always made my homecomings so nice – not least because you'd always bake me such a delicious cake – Papa gave me a letter from Inter-Aid saying that they've agreed to fund Wolfgang's ticket to Düsseldorf, so we'd only have to pay for his return trip. You can just imagine how thrilled I was, and now I'm certain that he'll be able to come. Papa sent him a postcard straight away with the good news, and I'm sure the time won't pass quickly enough for him.

I've just written to Frau Grünebaum to say that Hermann will definitely have a travelling companion at least as far as London, so she needn't worry. I also asked when it might suit her for me to visit – hopefully soon, before Wolfgang arrives – to hear all about what you've been up to.

Uncle Alfred now knows the name of the book you want. But tell me, is one allowed to send it? Also, I'm not quite sure that it's the right sort of book for you. Are there not more important things you might need? We can wait and see what Uncle Alfred says, but I don't think he'll be giving his enthusiastic approval.

This afternoon Eva-Maria has gone to see Grete Weyes, after she rang and wrote three times asking her to come. It's lovely how the old Bible Circle still tries to keep in touch with Eva-Maria.

Now, my dear child, keep well. Try not to be too miserable on Thursday, when everyone else leaves.

A big warm hug from Mama

Dear Edith! I still have work to do this evening, and since this letter has to go off in the post, I can't write more.

Heartfelt kisses from Papa

18 July 1937
Düsseldorf

FRIEDA TO EDITH

My love,

Do you know what? – I was expecting you all Thursday night until Friday morning. I had really imagined that you would come and surprise us all, and even though I kept telling myself that it was nonsense I became so obsessed by the idea that I actually managed to disappoint myself. I know of course that it would have been impossible for you to come, but how nice it would have been. So we'll just keep looking forward to Christmas, and it will be all the more lovely for the wait. – So you brought Hermann to London. I'll hear all about it from him on Saturday 24th, when I'll be in Elberfeld. We'll talk about you so much that your ears will burn. I always imagine that you are with me, and somehow you are, despite the distance between us. We're thrilled that we'll at least be seeing Wolfgang. Unfortunately Fräulein Grete is travelling herself this week, as she told me in a letter – otherwise I would have asked her to collect Wolfgang at Euston and deliver him to Victoria. Instead the poor boy has to make his own way, but I'm sure everything will work out.

I paid a visit to Frau Grossmann a few days ago and showed her your photos (which I always carry with me). She thought they were so nice, particularly the ones where you're laughing and picking flowers. If you could possibly send those two to her, please do so. I'm sure she'd be absolutely delighted with them. You could also write to Gert, who waits daily for the postman to bring him an answer to the letter he wrote to you in English, but in vain. It's touching to see how they're all so attached to you.

I would so like to keep on writing for hours, but I have too much work to do. I send you a big, big hug, my dear girl, and love from

Mama

18 July 1937
Düsseldorf

GEORG AND EVA-MARIA TO EDITH

My dear Mouse,

I'm delighted to learn from your letters that you're a bit happier, and taking things more at face value. Even Alfred Grünebaum, with whom I spoke recently about your dissatisfaction, thinks that what you're doing at the moment is the best solution, and that you should aim to speak the language perfectly, whatever happens. By the way, I can't share your enthusiasm for Shaw. Although I cannot deny that he has great spirit, to me he comes across as a rather stupid trade union secretary who happens to write. I find it wonderful that you're putting on 'little performances', as you describe them. How delighted Goethe would be if he knew – perhaps he does! – that his Leipzig student play is being performed for Germans in England, just as 'Hamlet' was staged in his 'Wilhelm Meister's Apprenticeship'. I hope the holidays are providing you with a bit of a change and the chance to relax.

Kisses from Papa

My dear old Clumsy Clot,

I'm sure you're thinking I'm a lazy swine for not having written to you. Well, that I certainly am, and I've got so much to tell you. Imagine this scene: last Sunday all the old Bible Circle folk were invited for the day to the Icherbicks' in Grimmstrasse. When we were all sitting round in a circle, I noticed that nearly everyone was wearing a ring. Just think, Erna Scheidemann has been married since January, and Inge Schmitz since 5 May! Can you imagine that? Friedel Lichtenfeld and Hanna Sebean are engaged. Grete Weyes' children are *so* sweet! Two boys with white-blond hair and blue eyes. One is quite big already, but the other is tiny. Herr Weyes is very friendly, and he told some marvellous jokes which I couldn't even begin to write down.

Now I have to tell you about something else. Uncle Alfred definitely wants to have me in Göttingen permanently, and to my great horror he's even found me a job there which starts on 1 October. Isn't that quite awful? What should I do? I'm really at a loss. Please don't mention this in your next letter, but maybe you could write me a note separately, OK? I've got to stop now. Everybody's looking over my shoulder as we've got to go out and this letter must go off today.

> 100000000000000000000 big fat kisses
> from your old Eva-Maria

> *1 August 1937*
> *Düsseldorf*

FRIEDA TO EDITH

My dearest Edith,

Now we're missing you dreadfully, but we think about you so much and talk about you constantly, so really you're with us all the time. I'm just looking forward to Christmas, and I hope so much that I'll have my trio together again then. In the end Inter-Aid bought Wolfgang a return ticket. Isn't that fabulous? He left Brackley at twenty to eight in the evening and a woman from Inter-Aid met him at Marylebone station in London. Then he was taken on a tour through London with two other German boys, and they sat and drank coffee before being put onto the train at eleven. He got here at midday and slept seventeen hours straight after I'd bundled him into bed quite against his will. Now he's enjoying his golden freedom, and he's so happy and jolly, just like in the old days.

It's been decided that Eva-Maria will go and live in Göttingen. In some respects it might be quite good for her. She's losing weight all the time here. In Göttingen she weighed 103 lb in her swimming costume and now, with a thick coat and hat on, she's only 100 lb. I beg you not to write to Uncle Alfred about any of this. We've finally made our minds up and I mustn't complain; instead I'll just hope that my children fulfil their responsibilities, wherever Fate has placed them, and that they build a life for themselves from there. – Have you remembered Uncle Alfred's birthday on 2 August? On 8 August it will have been a year since Aunt Martha died. I hope you've thought of writing to him – he's so generous towards you all, and he always involves himself in your lives. Now, my child, keep well.

A thousand kisses, Mama

2 August 1937
Düsseldorf

GEORG AND EVA-MARIA TO EDITH
Dear Edith,

We were over the moon to see Wolfgang again. He's just the same creature he was before, but much healthier and stronger. I am doing my best to make sure he doesn't forget his English, but in addition it seems he needs extra lessons in arithmetic and French, so that's what we're trying to arrange while he's here. You have to understand that it's just a temporary solution with Eva-Maria. There's no more news from this end really, and if there is I'm sure you'll find it in Mama's letter. At the moment I'm working on a lengthy legal treatise, and enjoying my work a great deal.

Many kisses from your Papa

Dear Edith,

You're right, I'm really dreadfully lazy when it comes to writing regularly. – It's such a shame that you're not here with us at the moment, but we're all so looking forward to Christmas. Wolfgang is terribly cheeky, perhaps even more so than before, but he's also big and brown and chubby. This whole Göttingen thing is such a dreadful mess. Whether I want to or not, I'm just going to have to be obedient and fall into line, and that's the worst of all. It's enough to drive you mad. But you shouldn't be spending any time worrying about it, and you can be sure that I will sort out everything here splendidly before I go, I promise. It's all perfectly insane, I mean, who comes first, Uncle Alfred or Mama and Papa? I scarcely need ask. Wolfgang won't be able to add anything today because he's been at the Rhine with the Hamachers all afternoon and isn't back yet. So my kisses come from Wolfgang too.

1000 big kisses from your old Eva-Maria

Georg's letter to Edith, 2 August 1937

10 August 1937
Düsseldorf

FRIEDA TO EDITH

My dear girl,

Your last letter was rather delayed because no one could decipher the address. It went on a tour of the whole of Düsseldorf before finally landing in Yorckstrasse. Looking at it, you could think it spelled the name of any other road in town – just not Yorckstrasse. Often your writing is so illegible that it's a real effort to read your letters. Do try to write a little clearer! Now 5 August has been and gone, and we thought of you and spoke about you so much, just as if you had been with us. The weather was so wonderful that we walked all the way to Grafenberg, and Eva-Maria joined us after work.

I still don't know when the Herzs are leaving, and now they're away for a few days. They wanted to set off between the 15th and 18th, and if she's feeling well enough Frau Herz will probably go too; recently she's been very ill indeed. Tomorrow afternoon I'm going to Frau Grossmann's for coffee. The children are in a day home and Grete has gone away, and the poor woman has so much to do. – Wolfgang is really enjoying his holidays: today he's at the bathing beach in Eller, and tomorrow he's going fishing on the Rhine with the Hamachers. He's become such a big, strong lad. Unfortunately he hasn't had any extra lessons since he's been here. Ruth [Schoen] has a permanent job now, so she doesn't have the time, and the other people we'd thought of have mostly gone away. Occasionally I read a bit of English with him, if I have the time.

Soon your life is going to start getting busy again, and then it's non-stop until Christmas! I only wish I knew how I could send you the fare for your trip, at least as far as the border. At the moment that's my biggest concern. – I have to get hold of all kinds of things for Wolfgang which he really needs for the winter, most importantly a decent quilt, and they seem to be awfully expensive. Do you need yours, or have you been given one by the school? You in particular need good warm blankets, as your kidneys and bladder seem to be so susceptible. It's so important that you look after yourself, my child.

With heartfelt kisses from your Mama

10 August 1937
Düsseldorf

GEORGE TO EDITH

Dear child,

Many thanks for your lovely birthday letter and the splendid presents, and for your letter of the 6th, which only arrived today. Because of your impeccable handwriting, the people at the post office read 'Gurckstrasse' instead of Yorckstrasse, and tried to find me there – in vain!

The wishes you sent me for my birthday touched me deeply, and with Carlyle's words you really hit the spot. His poem is quite splendid, particularly verses five to twelve. The photographs of you are beautiful. Wolfgang gave me an upright chrome photo frame, and now your large, serious image peers down onto my manuscripts while I'm working. The writing case is also quite lovely; I particularly like the front pocket of Japanese handmade paper – because of the political tension between Japan and China I can't now of course put a cup of Chinese tea next to it! In the end we didn't go to the Bauenhaus for my birthday, but to the Grafenberg woods instead. Wolfgang stood in for you, just as you asked, and on the way back got up to so much mischief that it nearly drove us mad. Here he's kept very busy swatting flies.

Uncle Alfred got an enlargement made of the photograph taken that time of you, Eva-Maria and Wolfgang in front of the dairy, and he gave it to me in a charming gold frame. I have it standing next to the picture of you on my writing desk. The birthday bunny certainly proved to be very generous this year.

My dear little Edith, many many thanks once again for everything.

Kisses from Papa

15 August 1937
Düsseldorf

PARENTS TO EDITH
My dear girl,

Your letter arrived punctually today, without going on a tour of the district, and I hope you're telling me the truth when you say you're really well. Frau Herz and Lore arrive on Wednesday. Lore will be bringing you everything you asked me for apart from the book, which we enclose here, as she's already sent off her baggage. Please do discuss everything that's on your mind with Frau Herz. She's such a lovely, kind person, and she will give you the best advice she can. Have you made any more plans? How long do you think you'll be able to stay on at Stoatley Rough? Please talk about all this and much more with Frau Herz. I am so glad that I'll be able to hear a bit more about you directly from her.

Of course it would have been wonderful if you had met up with Wolfgang in London, but I wouldn't have known how to arrange it. He only arrived there late at night, and I don't know where he could have stayed in order to see you the following day. Could you try to find out from an English timetable when the trains go from Marylebone station to Brackley? Frau Grossmann asked me to send the enclosed two letters on to you. I had a lovely time when I went to see her on Wednesday. We spoke about you a great deal, and I always love listening to the way people talk about you. Did you get the letter Gert wrote in English? He's been waiting such a long time for a reply.

I hope you've had enough good weather and fresh air for the holidays. It's pouring with rain today, so alas we won't be able to go for our planned walk. Keep well, my child, and please tell Frau Herz as much as you can about yourself. I want to know absolutely everything, and I'm so looking forward to her being able to tell me how you look.

Many kisses from your Mama

Dear child,

What I meant about the poem was that the central part is very good because it's written in convincing and unaffected language. The beginning and end, however, are affected and wooden. Despite this criticism, I find the poem as a whole positive and good; the irony is playful rather than malicious. I'm sorry I forgot to thank you for the leather pouch – it's beautifully made, and I'll use it for my keys. I so loved reading all about your studies! In a separate package I'm sending a Reklam edition of Hebbel's 'Herodes und Marianne'. Please look after it well – I bought it in Zurich in 1925 and used it for a literary study I was working on in Switzerland at the time. I also enclose a copy of Wolfgang's school report.

With many kisses,
Papa

23 August 1937
Düsseldorf

PARENTS TO EDITH
Dear child,

We've just received your lovely letter, and I want to jot down a few words in reply straight away as this afternoon I have to go to Elberfeld on a business matter. I can't wait to hear Frau Herz's account of your conversations. It's wonderful that Lore Herz is now at Stoatley Rough with you; she seems to be well liked by those who know her. The news that the Grünebaums are emigrating has not come as a complete surprise to us. Alfred Grünebaum is just the right kind of man to get ahead in America. His sister Mary has already emigrated with her second husband, and I'm assuming that she helped to arrange their passage over there. Hermann certainly has very good prospects, as they place great em-

phasis on the natural sciences in America. Despite the fact
that they're leaving, I'm so glad to have made contact with
them once more before they go – it's meant that I've got to
know Hermann (and he looks so like his late aunt, Hedwig!).

Many heartfelt kisses,

your Papa

My dear child,

I won't write much today as this letter has to go off, and
so do I. I am so very curious to hear what Frau Herz will
have to say about you and what you're up to, I can barely
wait until she's here. I worry endlessly about you and your
future. How many children are there at the school, now that
the holidays are over? Even if you don't get any more days
off, it can't be all that bad if you write that you often go
swimming, or walking.

Many kisses for today from your Mama

31 August 1937
Düsseldorf

FRIEDA TO EDITH

My dear child,

I've just got back from seeing Frau Herz, and she told me
all your news. The main thing is, how is your health now?
Has the whole thing really cleared up or will it keep recur-
ring? Also, it seems to be unclear what your next step should
be. How do you envisage things developing after you've
finished your dressmaking course? I definitely think (and

Papa agrees with me) that you should come back here for a
visit as soon as you can, but *on no account* should you stay.
For a thousand different reasons you would no longer feel
comfortable here, now that you've spent some time abroad.
There is no one of your age left, and the atmosphere here in
the house isn't exactly refreshing. As things now stand, just
about the only work available to you would be housekeeping, and that you can do over there of course. If you managed
to find a job in a good, cultured household, that might
perhaps be a way for you to get on in your career. Is that
Quaker address going to be of any help to you? They seem
particularly willing to help non-Aryans like ourselves, and if
they knew the circumstances they might take up your cause.
It is such a huge worry to me that I don't know what lies in
store for you in the future, and it would be such a relief if I
could see an opening for you somewhere. I am quite convinced that Fräulein Dr Lion will try to do as much as she can
for you; certainly that's what she promised to Frau Herz.

What do you think about coming home? It would cost
about 80 Marks via Southampton. We couldn't possibly
ask Uncle Alfred for that much; there's a limit to everything,
after all. Do you think there's a chance that the Quakers or
Inter-Aid might be able to help out? I'd only want to ask the
latter as a last resort as they're already being so generous
towards Wolfgang. How much is the fare in English
pounds? Return tickets are significantly cheaper; in fact
the return fare works out at only ten shillings more than a
one-way ticket. Best of all would be if you managed to find
a job before you came, so you'd know what you'd be going
back to, and that you could indeed go back. You don't have

to make your mind up overnight – there's still a bit of time.

I hope Lore is feeling better. I didn't mention her illness to her mother as I'm sure it was just a brief thing which will by now have passed. Do give her my best wishes. If she's homesick, or if there's anything else that's bothering her, she could always write to me. I could then let her mother know, without her worried father needing to hear about it. – It's wonderful that you're learning so much, and I'm glad that you're enjoying your lessons. Just keep warm so that you don't get ill.

It's three weeks before Wolfgang goes off again. I'm not sure he should take the train which gets into Victoria at nine in the evening; I can't imagine that he'll be able to get a connection to Brackley at that time of night. It's more likely that he'll leave here shortly after midnight and arrive in London at 4 p.m. I'd be grateful if you could look into the train times. Eva-Maria says she'll write to you next week, when she's finished work and has more time.

Big kisses and hugs from your Mama

31 August 1937
Düsseldorf

GEORG AND WOLFGANG TO EDITH
Dear Edith,

When Mama wrote to you with her thoughts about your future, she was writing on my behalf too. It's by no means a straightforward matter, nor are the possible solutions terribly satisfactory. But we can't do more than what we think is best. I'm sure your health will improve too; there doesn't seem to be anything serious to worry about on that front.

My legal treatise has just been accepted for publication by 'Geistiges Eigentum',* an intellectual periodical based in Leiden, near Amsterdam. At least the central part of it has, which is barely half. The piece as a whole has turned out to be rather substantial. In a few days I'll send two manuscripts to Fräulein Dr Wolf; she did invite me to do so after all. Do write and tell me what you think about all the issues relating to your future.

Warmest kisses from Papa

Dear Edith,

Yesterday we went to Ohligs in der Heide. It was so beautiful there, and afterwards we had lunch at the Engelsbergerhof restaurant. I go back to England in three weeks (worse luck!). The weather has sometimes been very nice. I'm now having private French lessons with a student.

Kisses from Wolfgang

6 September 1937
Düsseldorf

FRIEDA AND EVA-MARIA TO EDITH
My dear girl,

On the whole I'm sure you're right in what you say about your physical condition, but I'm still worried. I only hope I

---

* *Geistiges Eigentum* (literally 'intellectual property') specialised in copyright law.

don't have to wait too long for your visit; until I've taken a proper look at you I won't have any peace at all. Are you on any particular diet, and is there anything else you're doing for your health?

Have you now spoken to Fräulein Dr Lion about how long they plan to let you stay on there? That's the first thing we need to know. I imagine the prospects of a job at a school are not very good, but if a post were to come up it would certainly comply with my wishes for your future. I'm sure you'd quite enjoy it, and it's the kind of work that would suit you very well. It would do you the world of good to accept the invitation to go up to London one weekend. They could give you some very sound advice, and they only want to help out. Of course you shouldn't so openly declare what you don't like. Often dislikes have to be covered up. That's what life is like, and if you always say what's on your mind you might forfeit some things that are good. So do try to be a little wiser and more diplomatic than you normally are!

Now listen, I think you're entirely forgetting your German spelling. I've decided to correct you every time you misspell something, and you *must* take note: *Märchen* is not spelled with an *h* before the *r*, *eigentlich* doesn't have a *d*, *blendend* is without a *t*, and *Southampton* has a *p*. Please pay attention to all this, and try to improve it!

A thousand kisses from your Mama

My dear little sister,

Well, here comes my epistle. Today I'm at home all day for the first time – I've finished working in the office for good, and it's a very strange feeling. But at the end of the month I'm off to Göttingen, so I'm having my holidays now, before I go. I still haven't got my reference from Holländer, but it should be here by the end of the week and then I'll write to you again. My job has been filled by a 27-year-old girl who's never worked in an office and doesn't know how to do a single thing. – I imagine it must be splendid to have Lore over there with you.

Yesterday I went canoeing again with Jansenwirth – it was truly lovely and I got quite a tan. I think I'm rather a good canoeist now. This afternoon, whether I like it or not, I have to learn to ride a bicycle properly. My next epistle will be longer.

Lots of big fat kisses from Eva-Maria

6 *September 1937*
Düsseldorf

GEORG TO EDITH

Dear Edith,

What you wrote about your health in your last letter largely reassured me. Unfortunately you have partly inherited your low energy levels and this tendency to founder from me. In fact my heart isn't quite developed, so I've suffered from abnormal degrees of tiredness ever since I was a young man. It's always been disturbingly apparent to me, but there's nothing that can be done about it.

From your letter I gather that you are also concentrating on expanding your intellect, as well as doing your housekeeping work. This was, of course, wonderful to hear, and your English teacher appears to be a quite excellent individual. It goes without saying that you shouldn't overexert yourself in that area either.

I hope so much that you will be able to come over and see us for a while soon. Even if you haven't found yourself a permanent post, you should still ensure that you're getting your holidays. Wolfgang leaves us again in about fourteen days, and Eva-Maria soon after.

More loving kisses from your Papa

10 September 1937
Düsseldorf

GEORG TO EDITH

Dear child,

Many thanks for your lovely letter! I don't think it's such a tragedy that those particular sections of the Oedipus manuscript have not been understood by everybody. I am used to the fact that only a few people will ever understand my lectures, even though I do try to force myself down to a more 'popular' level. Since I write with such seriousness I suppose I can't expect anything else, particularly if the audience consists of such young ladies – I certainly can't hold this against them. In any case this manuscript is only the first and much shorter half of my complete work on 'King Oedipus', as I explained to Fräulein Dr Wolf in my letter. In the second half, which you could say is the more theoretical part, I explore the fundamental problems in this particular tragedy, and in the genre itself. I can read this second part to you when you're here at Christmas, if you don't find it too exhausting.

As far as the novella is concerned, you seem to have grasped a great deal of it. But it's also to do with something completely different: what I'm trying to say is that life in all its mundane detail and manifestations is irrelevant; the only thing worth striving for is a union with the most profound laws of existence. One philosopher, I think it was Lotze, named one of his books 'Zur Einheit mit dem Unendlichen' ['Thoughts on a Union with the Infinite'], and this is the concept which informs me and my entire life, and which I am trying to express in this novella. In his book about Goethe, Gundolf, in contrast to Spinoza's pantheism of the natural world, outlines the 'pantheism of history', using Herder as an example. This historical pantheism is expressed in what my novella has to say about the work that Marianen's father does. On reading these words, certain well-informed Thebans will declare that my novella is contrived on the basis of abstract concepts. The truth of the matter is that I set down the novella quite simply to satisfy my own needs, and only later, as I was pondering its meaning, did I come to this conclusion.

Many kisses from Papa

PS I enclose your first vaccination certificate, but I still have to find the second. If you need it before we send off our next letter, please write me a card saying so.

13 September 1937
Düsseldorf

GEORG AND EVA-MARIA TO EDITH

Dear Edith,

We are so glad that the news on your health is ultimately reassuring. With any luck the other issues will be settled to all our satisfaction in the discussion you'll soon be having with Fräulein Dr Lion. I've packed up the manuscripts for Fräulein Dr Wolf and they're ready to go off. Should I send them to her directly, or to you? What is her exact address?

Many heartfelt kisses from Papa

My dear little Edith,

Here it's terribly cold, just like in the office when there's no heating. It's a real nuisance as we'd planned so many nice outings together. We thought we'd be able to get really brown, the two of us, but now we're just sitting around at home.

By the way, I got a very respectable reference from Holländer. My successor is quite daft. In the evenings I do some bookkeeping at home with Jansenwirth. He's showing me all the basics so that I have a bit of an idea later on. – I went into town yesterday morning with Ruth [Schoen] and Hilde [Wegner], and that was great fun. Even more fun are my endless trips (with Wolfgang) to Zimpel, the dentist. He's already pulled a tooth and given me lots of fillings. I have to say, it's been a real pleasure. But it'll all be done soon, thank God.

I think it's marvellous that you have such enjoyable

evenings from time to time. You must have learned so much there already, and I'm sure it will stay all with you for the rest of your life. Unfortunately I'm hardly reading at all these days – I just don't seem to get round to it, but I bet you know all about that. At the moment I'm dipping into Johann Christof von Romain Rolland.

Have you written to the Grossmanns yet? Mama's going to visit them this week, and she so wanted you to send them a letter before she gets there. I'll probably be setting off for Göttingen in two weeks today. Please write me a separate note of what you'd like sent from there (from Uncle Alfred) so that you get what you really want and need. That's enough for now; Jansenwirth is on his way for some more bookkeeping.

Lots of big fat kisses from your Eva-Maria

15 September 1937
Göttingen

ALFRED COHN TO EDITH
Dear Edith,

Three days ago I returned from a four-week stay at a sanatorium in Wildungen. I regularly get news of you as your parents forward your letters, and I always read them with a great deal of pleasure. I hope you will manage to accomplish everything that you are striving for with so much strength of will. Only try to be a little more reticent in the future about communicating your various minor accidents and bouts of illness. You know very well that your mother is gifted in the art of making mountains out of molehills just by building things up in her mind. I'm not saying in the least that your ailments are all molehills, but I do know what a strong will can wrest from a body when it won't obey the spirit.

I was interrupted at this point, and now I've just received your letter. You say that you are quite happy, and have no particular wishes beyond those that you feel it would be impertinent to ask for. But might there not be one impertinence that I could send you from here? If you really can't think of anything, we'll have to discuss it at some point. It does, however, have to be within the bounds of possibility. Otherwise in the end you'll come to me with the request that I acquire a London theatre for you, so that you can perform a starring role there. When I was a young man I used to wish for things like that too. Actually I wanted to write for the theatre, but I soon realised that this wasn't at all what the Lord our God had intended for me, so I tried to get something out of life by other means. You too seem to have realised that the best you can do with your ambitions is to give Fate (should she ever prove sympathetic) every available opportunity to implement your plan for you, that is to say to try to learn as much as you can so that when the time comes you'll be able to declare in as many different situations as possible: My master, thy vessel is prepared.*

I would be so happy to hear from you again sometime.
        With very best regards from Uncle Alfred

---

* Refers to passage in the Bible, 2 Timothy 2:21 '. . . he shall be a vessel unto honour, sanctified, and meet for the master's use, and prepared unto every good work'.

29 September 1937
Düsseldorf

GEORG TO EDITH [incomplete]
My dear child,

I found your letter waiting for me on my return from Amsterdam. There are very obvious grounds for not writing to you from there. The reason for my trip was to have a meeting with the people at the periodical 'Geistiges Eigentum', which as you know will be publishing my latest legal essay. I've just been commissioned to write a second, and I'm planning a third, which I haven't yet discussed with the editor. In addition I've been entrusted with the task of reporting on German periodicals, and highlighting articles in them which might be of interest to 'Geistiges Eigentum'. I can now regard myself as an employee of the periodical, and it definitely seems to be on the ascent; it has even established an editorial office in New York. The financial return is extremely modest, but not entirely inconsiderable, and the main thing in any case is its influence and the possibility it affords me to make contacts.

Now, as far as the tone of my letters is concerned, I was not aware that you found them rather too businesslike and superficial (apart from the two most recent ones). This is just the way I write, and I share it with many other people who have no lack of personal emotions just because they are not inclined to display them in their letters; I must remind you that you've often noted and emphasised this same quality in the letters you've received from your uncle in Göttingen. I am sure there are not many fathers who are as involved as I am in what their children are doing, or as interested in everything they have to say, right down to the last detail. Not everyone would have supported their children the way I do. If I don't always refer to your personal problems, it's because Mama does so constantly, and of course she speaks on behalf of us both after we've discussed the issues in question. It seems to me to be pointless for both of us to write to you about the same things. It didn't occur to me at all to criticise the fact that you postponed your discussion with Fräulein Dr Lion, and equally ridiculous is the idea that I imagine you to be indifferent to your own progress. If I suggested that your discussion should take place as soon as possible, it's because I thought it might mean that you could come and see us all the sooner.

In my last letter but one I asked you all kinds of questions about how to send over the manuscripts, and because of the subject I adopted a particularly businesslike tone. In that letter I also asked whether I should send the manuscript to you, or directly to Fraülein Dr Wolf, and I wanted you to give me her address. And finally, I specifically asked you to respond to all – and I underlined that word – of my questions; I was of course irritated that you didn't do so, so I may have been a little short with you in my last letter . . .

29 September 1937
Düsseldorf

FRIEDA TO EDITH

My dear girl,

What a shame that you didn't get to see Wolfgang! He's brought all kinds of things over for you, but I expect he'll send them to you soon. The poor lad has somehow got himself a kidney stone, and sometimes he seems to be in real pain. We're all hoping that in time it will pass of its own accord, so that he won't need an operation. Because of this my heart was so much the heavier to see him leave us again, but that's how it has to be. I was worried that he might lose his place at the school if he stayed here any longer. – We were so happy to hear that you'd spent such wonderful days in London, but in the end the most important thing is that you were given some good advice, and that the people there were able to help you out in some way. Even with the best will in the world there's simply nothing we can do for you from here.

My thoughts circle constantly around the three of you and your futures. It is simply devastating to realise that I will no longer have any involvement at all in the way your lives develop. I'll just have to learn to accept everything as it comes. – Eva-Maria left yesterday. I don't really want to go into it now. How or even whether I'll be able to bear it and endure this loneliness I just don't know!

It's possible that we'll be seeing you before we see the others. My, how we'll enjoy being together again. Even though we have always had this deep sense of unity, I feel we have been all the more aware of just how much we love each other since we've been physically separated. Don't you agree, my little girl? I think it's wonderful that you have to write your main essay in English. It's a shame you're not typing it out, because you could have sent me a carbon, and one of your Lessing essay too. All this is a healthy counter-balance to the practical work you have to do besides, and it must do you an awful lot of good, even if you might be thinking now that you would be better off using your time more practically.

I must stop for today – I'm dead tired! Sleep well and sweet dreams! Do you pray at night??

Loving kisses,
Mama

PS I enclose a transcript of Eva-Maria's reference, just so you can see what sort of a sister you have!

6 October 1937
Düsseldorf

PARENTS TO EDITH

Dear child,

Today I'll be writing most of this letter, as Mama has made herself available for the occasional half-day to do temporary work at Holländers. Eva-Maria's successor was sacked for being completely incompetent, and they haven't yet found a replacement. Mama is working there for the first time today, on a trial basis, so she won't have time to write to you at any length, and we didn't want you or Wolfgang to have to wait longer than usual for your letters.

We were so happy to read your last letter. You are very fortunate that Fräulein Dr Lion is looking after your interests; we find her conduct extremely noble and generous, and we thoroughly approve of the advice she's given you so far. Do you think she'll be able to make any headway with the Quakers on your behalf? Whatever happens I am assuming that you'll be coming over before Christmas for quite a long stay, and I look forward to it very much. Wolfgang is now under medical treatment, with a certain Dr Gerald Stathers in Brackley. Dr Schöndorff has sent him the X-rays and the results of his tests. According to Wolfgang, it seems that the stone has started to move and will probably be passed before long. It appears that Mrs Bolton is doing what she can, and she even gave us a detailed report in German. I think it would still be a great comfort to Wolfgang if you could speak to him from Oxford. By the way, he still writes that he's managing to keep up at school. I just hope it's true!

Thank you for confirming receipt of my manuscripts. I haven't yet heard anything from Fräulein Dr Wolf. Obviously I would be delighted if she chose to read out passages from the Oedipus text. Do ask her for the text of the novella and read it through. I have been asked by 'Geistiges Eigentum' to review foreign magazines as well, but of course I'll only be considering those published in French. I enclose the copy of Eva-Maria's reference.

Warmest kisses,

Papa

My dear girl,

I'm adding a few short lines so that you get a little greeting from me too. I can't write much though, I'm dead tired: I worked all morning until one, and this afternoon I spent four and a half hours in the office. It's a little too much, but work is the best antidote. It's wonderful news that you'll be able to stay on there until Christmas! Let's just hope you can stay in England after that too.

A thousand kisses,
Mama

10 October 1937
Düsseldorf

FRIEDA TO EDITH

My dear child,

I'm glad your letter arrived today, Sunday, and not on Monday, as it mostly has been recently. This means that I'll at least have time to write to you, as it's getting much more difficult to do so in the week. My time is more than taken up. Since I don't have anyone to help with the deliveries, I'm often only at home after one, and then I quickly have to cook and have lunch to get to the office by three. Of course it's all rather exhausting, but the extra income is extremely welcome. Because of poor business and Wolfgang's illness and so on, I've rather fallen into arrears, but now I'll at least be able to catch up a bit. And then I'll start saving too so that we can all have a lovely Christmas without too many worries and constraints. I can't wait to see how everything will turn out, and especially how your prospects develop. The administrative work at Holländers is just temporary and could end any day, but then I'll certainly make an effort to look for something else. I'm trying to learn as much as I can, and I've already managed to grasp the basics of filing etc. I imagine I'd be able to take on a fairly undemanding office job with a good conscience.

Eva-Maria now seems to be enjoying life in Göttingen a bit more, and I can only be glad if in your letters the three of you sound more or less happy and content. I think it best that we have a particular day for post from each of you. Wolfgang's letter arrives punctually Tuesdays, Eva-Maria's on Thursdays, and I always look forward to yours on a Sunday. When it doesn't come then, which is often, the whole day seems much longer than normal.

I can imagine that you were thrilled about the photographs. Herr Kaumann took one of Eva-Maria on the last day she was here, and it turned out very well. I'll send you a print of it next week. Now listen, child, what has become of your spelling? You have to be quite tough with yourself and try to get it right: *eigentlich* is not spelled with a *d*, and *während* has an *h*. It's what struck me most about your last letter, and I'm afraid it's something you're just going to have to learn – it certainly doesn't do you any favours.

Today I'm going to spend the entire day darning and mending, and I'll be able to let my thoughts wander. They go off on long trips here and there. Sometimes they're in England, sometimes in Germany, and then I imagine that the door will open any minute, and in will come my three children, laughing and singing and acting the fool. I so hope I'll be able to hear that again sometime soon! There are so many children now who don't have parents, and it's a different experience for each individual. There's no pattern!

– Now I'm already looking forward to next Sunday, when I'll get another lovely letter from you.

Kisses from Mama

18 October 1937
Düsseldorf

FRIEDA TO EDITH [incomplete]

My dear girl,

Thank you for today's letter. I really wasn't aware that I'd expressed so much of my sorrow last time I wrote, and certainly not to the extent that you could feel burdened by it. I readily admit that what you say is basically right, and I'll certainly try to give it some thought. But I can't promise that anything will come of it. Believe me, the hard work that dominates my life at the moment is the only remedy, the most effective antidote against everything else. It hasn't yet been decided how much longer I'll be able to work at the office. At any rate I was delighted to receive my wages for the week, sixteen Marks ten, and I immediately plugged a large hole with it.

Your intention to work half-days here in the holidays is not an option – neither Papa nor I will allow it. We'll be so unbelievably happy to have our girl all to ourselves for a change, and the last thing we'd want to do is give you up to other people for half the day. No, it's completely out of the question, and I don't want to hear you mention it ever again. When you're here I'll even let you boss me about a bit – I know how much you enjoy it – and then I'll be very good and obediently fall into line . . .

31 October 1937
Düsseldorf

FRIEDA TO EDITH

My dearest Edith,

I hardly dare believe that I only have six more letters to write before I can kiss and hug you for real! And yet every time I look forward to your arrival – which I do with all my heart – a little question keeps popping up: What then? If only I could see a solution to the problem!

It's not at all nice that you now have to share a room with such unsuitable companions. I hope your conversations don't lead to any unpleasant situations. Ultimately it can only be a good thing to learn to understand the viewpoints of people who think differently and, where necessary, to use these differences to help strengthen and sharpen your own opinions. But the first consideration should always be: tolerance and respect for the viewpoints of others rather than arrogantly sticking to your own. If you adopt this attitude when you discuss your differences of opinion, only good can come of it.

I still don't know when I'll finish working at the office, but whenever it is I'll go to Berlin for a few days and on the way back spend a Sunday in Göttingen. I'm in urgent need of a rest. The business in the morning and then office work in the afternoon have rather exhausted me. I'm going to do absolutely nothing today and tomorrow (All Saints' Day), so that I can go to work on Tuesday with renewed vigour.

Lore is in London today for the Gigli concert, so her mother tells me. I hope she thoroughly enjoys it. With any luck you two will be able to travel back together for

Christmas! – So, my treasure, I'm going to close for today. December 26th, Wolfgang's birthday, is only eight weeks away! I wonder how Christmas will be, and whether we'll all be together again.

A big hug and a kiss from Mama

1 November 1937
Düsseldorf

GEORG TO EDITH

My dear Pup,

I'm so sorry not to have been able to hear your talk on Goethe. I'm afraid I have to be a little brief on the personal side today as I'm so busy with my new legal treatise. At some point I've got to return four books to the library and so far I've worked my way through only two of them.

Now I have to move on to the following important matter: as you know, your passport runs out in February 1938. In order to extend it, you will have to make an application to the appropriate German consulate in England. You'll have to apply straight away; usually it takes an age to come through. It will have to be sorted out at this end too, before you leave, or you'd have to cut short your visit in order to be back in England before your current passport expires. As far as I can determine from here, the German Consulate General in London would be responsible for the Haslemere area. Try to find out about all this at the school, and also ask them whether you will have to make your application for the extension personally or in writing; they should know all this from previous applications. Also, try to discover whether you will need a certificate from the BDM.* The local passport office said you wouldn't, but I wasn't entirely convinced by this. When you've made your application to the consulate, they'll ask the local office here (the police headquarters) if there are any reasons not to grant the extension. In the meantime I'll facilitate the passport office's decision by obtaining the required documents from the various tax offices that show you are no cause for concern. So, let's get to work!

Loving kisses from your old Pa

PS I enclose your vaccination certificate.

7 November 1937
Düsseldorf

FRIEDA TO EDITH

My dear little Edith,

Is it really true that in fourteen days you will be here, bringing into our house the joy that we have lacked for such a long time!?! I can hardly believe that there will be laughter here in this very room, and that I will hear the word 'Mama'! The thought of it is just too, too lovely! And then there's also the possibility of an apprenticeship! It sounds too good to be true. What do they mean by 'probation'? Would it be a free place, or how would it work? From what I've heard, people who complete their apprenticeship at a children's home like that one are given work permits automatically. When would the training there begin?

---

* National Socialist organisation for girls, equivalent to the Hitler Youth.

Your passport has to be extended over in England because you are registered as being abroad. If you have to be back over there before your passport expires you would still be meeting the requirements if you had it extended after your return. At the moment it remains a complete mystery to me how the whole trip will work out. Papa is going to the foreign exchange office here, but it's rather doubtful that he'll be allowed to buy the ticket. Don't you think the Quakers might be able to help you get the ticket, if it came to that? Isn't it much more expensive if you go via the Hook of Holland?

I'm glad to hear that it's not so bad in your room after all. Didn't I say that with a bit of wit and goodwill even the most difficult situations can turn out well!

My love, I hope that the miniature Martinmas lamp will remind you of all our jolly Martinmas evenings. I've made one for each of you, but unfortunately I can't send any sweets with it. You'll be able to have twice as much when you're here. Please let us know as soon as you have news, whatever the decision.

                    A big hug and kisses from Mama

                                    8 November 1937
                                    Düsseldorf

GEORG TO EDITH
Dear Edith,

We're delighted that you will be here soon, and perhaps very soon indeed. I entirely approve of your plan for what should happen next in England, so you can ignore your application for a passport extension for the time being. There's really nothing to report from here. Apart from going about the unavoidable daily chores, I am doing nothing other than devoting myself exclusively to my work, which, divided as it is into two areas, takes up a great deal of my time and energy.

Hopefully your next letter will tell us more about your plans for the future and how they are developing, and of course when exactly you're coming to see us.

Kisses from Papa

In November 1938, Edith learned that she had been offered an apprenticeship at St Mary's Home for Disabled Children in Horam, Sussex, so her family in Düsseldorf prepared for her to visit for a few days in early December rather than at Christmas.

28 November 1937
Düsseldorf

GEORG TO EDITH

My dear Puppy,

That is simply splendid news! Of course we can't quite imagine it all, and we eagerly await further news from you. In the meantime we're mobilising ourselves here so that we can receive you with the appropriate salute of honour, and we've stored up large quantities of antidotes in case you intend to test out your newly acquired cooking skills! Incidentally, since I last wrote I submitted my complete report on German periodicals to the editorial department, and I've already heard that it's going to be published.

Many kisses from Papa

28 November 1937
Düsseldorf

FRIEDA TO EDITH

My dearly beloved girl,

I am so happy to know that you are now beginning to sort out a life for yourself that will, in all probability, be purposeful and fulfilling. Now I can hardly wait for the moment when I will be able to hold you tight in my arms, and appreciate again that my little girl is a creature I can touch and see, who doesn't only exist at an unobtainable distance, in letters. To be quite honest, the joy of having you here quite dominates everything else at the moment. Of course it's hard that you can only be here for such a short time, but we won't let that spoil our utter joy at seeing you. Who was the sponsor of this happiness? Did you get the money through the Quakers? Anyway, you'll soon be able to tell us all about it in person.

We will always be hugely indebted to Fräulein Dr Lion; without her, and ultimately without the help of Fräulein Poensgen, you'd never have got this far. But of course this has only come about because you've fulfilled all your duties extremely well there – otherwise they would never have accepted you at the new school. So in the end you only have yourself to thank for what you've achieved, and in life that is almost always the case. In the circumstances don't you think it would be better to get yourself a return ticket, if that's possible? I've already written to Uncle Alfred about all this.

I've just been speaking to Frau Herz. If you don't have too much to carry, she's asked whether you could bring back some things from Lore. We still haven't heard whether Wolfgang will be able to come for Christmas or not. We might even be on our own! – What do you want me to cook on the day you arrive? Please write and tell me what you'd like most, and what kind of cake. It'll be the first I've baked since Eva-Maria left! I'm quite dotty with excitement. Please give my regards to Fräulein Dr Lion, Wolf, etc., etc. I won't write to them until I've heard more about everything from you. So, all the best for your journey, and please be careful. Don't get seasick. According to our little timetable, you should be here at about 11.30. The kisses I intend for you will soon be delivered in person.

With all my love,
Mama

19 December 1937
Düsseldorf

PARENTS TO EDITH

Dear Edith,

Wolfgang has just written to say that he won't be coming home. In case he doesn't give you the address soon, I'm writing it here so that you can send his things off to him in time. Wolfgang Lindemeyer, c/o Miss Bliss, Melverley, Wimbourne, Dorset. I'm sure he could do with the warm pullover while he's there. I'll send him the other things in two one-lb parcels.

Now I'm curious to hear how you're settling in there. It was wonderful of Ilse Kleinertz to put sweets next to your bed. I could love the girl just for that. – I hope she's friendly otherwise, and a good companion for you. I'm glad you survived the trip without incident, and even more delighted that you didn't starve on the way. Today – Sunday – I keep thinking: this time last week!!! Your stay passed so incredibly quickly, but still, we must be glad and grateful that it all worked out the way it did. I doubt you'll be able to meet up with Wolfgang during the holidays. The poor lad, spending both Christmas *and* his birthday amongst strangers for the first time. Now imagine this: Frau von Baeyer has just been by plane from London to Düsseldorf, and it only took two and three-quarter hours! I find it most reassuring to know that we could be with you so soon if necessary, if there was an emergency.

At the moment our preparations for Christmas are in full swing. It's so much work, but I've nearly got it all organised. I hope we'll soon be hearing all about your new surroundings in detail!

Loving kisses from Mama

Dear Edith,

I keep thinking about how lucky you are to be living in your current circumstances. I am so glad we had the opportunity to talk everything through; I think we managed to clear up a few issues, and more than just theoretically too

. . . It's hard that Wolfgang will now be staying over there for the holidays, and particularly hard for him. I hope you're happy with the way things are going there, and that you're not having to work too hard.

Kisses from Papa

Eva-Maria and Edith, c. 1932

1938

6 January 1938
Düsseldorf

FRIEDA TO EDITH

My dear Edith,

We so loved getting your letter, and everything in it is described so well and clearly that sometimes I think I'm right there in the middle of it all. Now, do you want thick or thin black stockings? If you let me know I'll send them immediately, and tell me at the same time if there's anything else you need. Maybe there's something in particular you'd like for when you're both together on the 17th?

I'm sure it's sometimes difficult for you, having to work so hard, but I can also see from your letters that you enjoy what you're doing, and that you're having a wonderful time with everyone else who's there. I'm so glad about that. It makes such a tremendous difference who one works with, and I have the impression that I don't need to worry about you in that respect. The performances you put on must be great fun, and if you're able to laugh as much as all that, then there can be no room for feelings of sadness. That has to be worth a great deal. – I think it's quite splendid that you're meeting up with Wolfgang on the 17th. Please send me a long and detailed letter afterwards, telling me how he is. Will you both be seeing Fräulein Grete? Have you heard anything more about your passport renewal? Please don't neglect the issue.

We spent the days over Christmas very quietly at home. I just stayed in bed, which is just what I really needed, but now I'm working again. At the moment I'm knitting a romper suit somebody has ordered. That's why you'll have to be content with this short letter for today, as I have to get it finished soon.

A thousand kisses,
Mama

PS Do you think you'll be able to go to Inter-Aid on the 17th, to talk to them about the confirmation, etc? You could find out what they think, and what their intentions are as far as he's concerned. He *has* to be confirmed – the only question is where!

12 January 1938
Düsseldorf

FRIEDA TO EDITH

My dear girl,

I was delighted when your dear letter arrived as I wasn't really expecting it. I'd got used to the fact that it rarely arrives on a Sunday any more, so it was all the more lovely that it blew in yesterday morning. I think I almost know my way around your new environment. You've described it in such detail that I can picture everything before me quite precisely, but I'd so like to be able to see my foster-grandchild properly. What sort of a little chap is he? You don't explain at all why he's there with you; what's actually the matter with him? I'm so happy for you that Ilse Kleinertz is such a sweet thing. Even if she's younger than you, it's still lovely that the only girl there from this neck of the woods is so nice. It's wonderful that you can have so much fun, despite all the work you have to do, and that life can still be a pleasure – it's so important to have this kind of counterbalance to your work.

I'll be sending off your stockings either tomorrow or the day after. The weather here is so dreadful that I am only running my work errands, which I have no choice but to do. I enclose a letter sent by Miss d'Avigdor to Mr Bolton, which Wolfgang has forwarded to us. In it she writes that Wolfgang will only need a passport at the end of his fifteenth year, but that's not when he's sixteen, as she explains, but rather when he's fifteen, because that's when his fifteenth year has passed. So he should be applying for it right away. Papa got the same information from the passport office here. Because the whole process takes such a long time, we really must set about it as soon as possible. You haven't given me an answer about your own passport situation. These issues are so incredibly important; they simply cannot be put off. – I'll probably be going off to Berlin for a few days soon, and afterwards to Göttingen for two more days. Bergenthal thinks it very important that I get some rest. It's not much, but it's better than nothing. – I hope you have really good weather on Monday, and a truly wonderful day.

A thousand kisses from Mama

17 January 1938
Düsseldorf

FRIEDA TO EDITH [incomplete]

My dear child Edith,

For once I'd so like to be a little mouse – I'll be with you in my thoughts for the whole of today. I hope you will send me an extremely precise account of what you get up to, with every detail and all the rows, etc. I want to know how Wolfgang looks, how he behaves, whether he's been biting his nails, whether his hair is short and his teeth are clean. – I only hope the whole passport business works out. When are you thinking of going to see Miss d'Avigdor? If she asks whether we want to sacrifice Wolfgang's summer visit (since he'll now be coming back for his confirmation anyway), it would be best if you told her that you want to speak to us about it first. Then I'll take your letter with this question to Pastor Homann, and I'll ask him whether in the circumstances he might confirm Wolfgang on his own in summer after all.

One more thing: I haven't passed on your letter to Frau Grossmann, because of course you really should know by now that it's her birthday on 27 January. She is so attentive to you, and so kind to me, that I simply have to ask you to send her a particularly nice birthday letter to arrive punctually on the day, and if possible enclose a pretty little flower too. You know how sensitive she is about things like that, and I'm really very fond of her.

It's terribly sad that I'm going to have to give up my foster-grandchild again so quickly. But maybe there'll be another soon. You'll have to write and let me know immediately. It's certainly much better for the child if he's back with his real mother, because there's no substitute for that. I just can't understand how anyone would want to separate themselves from their child of their own free will, and still less if the child is sick. I always find that an ill child pulls at your heartstrings all the more.

Since I have your letter next to me here, as I always do, I'm going through it bit by bit. My trip is coming up soon and, yes, I'm going to be extremely frivolous and set off as early as 28 January, first to Göttingen and then on to Berlin on the 31st for two weeks, until after Aunt Bertha's birthday. I feel very bad about leaving Papa alone for such a long time, but I think and hope that I'll be much fresher and more able-bodied when I get back . . .

19 January 1938
Düsseldorf

GEORG TO EVA-MARIA [incomplete]
Dear Eva-Maria,

A few days ago I called in on Dr Bergenthal to talk to him about Mama's condition. He assured me that she definitely doesn't have a physical heart defect, and he repeated this statement despite my persistent questioning. The existing symptoms, and particularly the heart murmurs, can be attributed to Mama's age, and to the obvious changes that take place in a woman's body during those years. It's not known for sure where these problems stem from, so we have to assume for the time being that they start in the kidneys. Similar symptoms are being observed in all cases like hers, albeit with very different degrees of gravity.

Physical exhaustion and emotional upset have also contributed to it. More than anything, the fact that she had to separate from all three of her children in the space of eight months must have been crucial. Anyone would be able to predict with almost mathematical certainty the effect that this must have on a woman, and especially one who is a mother with every fibre of her personality and being. Subjectively, this situation is very bad for the patient, but objectively it gives no cause for concern, and certainly there's no reason to think that it might be dangerous. Of course you know that I don't exactly think Bergenthal is a genius, and nor it seems does anyone else. But the fact that he denied any possibility of a physical heart defect, despite my repeated questioning, seems to me to be significant. If he had any doubt at all he wouldn't have denied it, as then he would be burdening himself with a huge responsibility . . .

25 January 1938
Düsseldorf

PARENTS TO EDITH

My dear child,

Even though your letter arrived two days late, this was compensated for by its content and length. Your description of Wolfgang pleased me more than anything. It's wonderful that you two spent such a lovely day together, and Wolfgang wrote about the day with such enthusiasm too. I'm particularly glad to know that he now has quite serious plans for the future, and doesn't just go through life without thinking. For him it's probably much better that he looks at life soberly, and tries to cut out that hereditary sentimentality. Anyway, your letter did me a great deal of good in every respect. I now plan to set off on Friday lunchtime, first of all to Berlin and to Göttingen only on the 12th, the day after Aunt Bertha's birthday. I have so much to get done today as, quite apart from the business which I've sorted out in advance for the time I'm away, I've got all kinds of things to arrange for the trip, and no Edith here to help me. If it wasn't completely clear to me that I desperately need this rest, I wouldn't be going, but I will be happy if the trip does for me what it's supposed to! – Of course you needn't write to both of us while I'm away. Just send your letters here as usual. Papa can then send them straight on to me, and in Berlin your letters will be my only *real* joy.

A big hug and warm kisses from your Mama
PS I think you're right about the confirmation, so whatever happens we'll have to give up the idea of 13 March. But then when and where will it be possible?!

Dear Edith,

We could tell from your letter that your day with Wolfgang was pleasurable and harmonious. According to your description the boy must have matured a great deal. I'll certainly send him a German book, if I can afford to, and I'll let you know so that you can try to persuade him to read it too. I haven't got much to report at this end. I'm continuing with my writings on art and science, and I have the feeling that I'm beginning to make some progress.

Loving kisses, Papa

31 January 1938
Düsseldorf

PARENTS TO EDITH

Dear child,

Thank you for your wonderful letter! I got it yesterday morning, before I left for Essen to visit the Folkwang Museum, and today I'm sending it on to Berlin for Mama. I know you're not having an easy time, and I'm sure your lessons are sometimes extremely difficult. But the way you describe them, it sounds as though they are intended to give you a very rounded education, and above all to integrate you even further into the English way of life. Is Wolfgang's voice really breaking? What a momentous event!

Enclosed you'll find the letter of consent you asked for. I've ordered the three notebooks from Hamacher and I'll probably be able to send them off tomorrow. And as far as the dress is concerned, Mama's told me to make a note in my diary for 8 February to ask the Herzs whether Lore is going to be travelling, and to give her the dress if that suits.

Loving kisses,
your Papa

My dear little Edith,

To save on postage Papa has sent his letter here, and I'll make sure I'm quick so that you get it soon. I've been here since Friday afternoon but, as with everything, I've had the most terrible bad luck here too. Since yesterday morning Aunt Bertha has been in bed with suppurating tonsillitis and a high temperature. This isn't exactly going to do my own convalescence any good, as you can imagine. The doctor came yesterday and again today, and he's doing what he can to speed up her recovery. – I loved your letter. Even if you're not always finding it easy, you're obviously enjoying your work and really benefiting from the teaching. That counts for an awful lot.

I am so thrilled to hear all your positive news about Wolfgang. I just wish I could get to see him again! Fräulein Dr Lion will be in Berlin for the next few days, and I'll go and pay her a visit. Unless you don't think that's such a good idea? If you don't, then please quickly send me a postcard by return. I think it would be the right thing to do, at any rate.

Uncle Richard was here today. It seems you didn't thank him for the little package he sent you. Please make up for it as soon as possible. You could of course enclose a note in a letter to me, to save on postage. – It's Uncle Josi's birthday on Thursday (the 3rd), and Aunt Bertha's on the 11th. I hope all these celebrations won't be spoilt by Aunt Bertha's illness. *Everyone* sends their love.

A huge hug from Mama

8 February 1938
Berlin

FRIEDA TO EDITH
Dear little Edith,

I was most of all happy to hear that they are pleased with you at St Mary's. That's the way it goes, you see: they demand a great deal of you, but one day they acknowledge it. I tried to visit Dr Lion in Apostel-Paulus Strasse this morning, only to be told that she hadn't in the end come back to Berlin, but that Dr Wolf was in Hewald Strasse. After I'd taken various buses and ended up in areas I didn't know, I couldn't find her there either. I spoke to her parents and left my card with some lovely branches of lilac. I'm so sorry that I didn't get to speak to anybody, but it couldn't be helped. They're leaving for England again tomorrow. Please don't neglect to get in touch with them, and don't ever forget what you have to thank them for! – Of course it's a lovely idea that you plan to meet up with Wolfgang again so soon, and I can quite understand that you want to, but I don't think it's justifiable to be spending your money like that. It's two weeks' wages! If people realise that's where your money is going they might stop offering to help you out, or Wolfgang either for that matter. And I'm certain there will come a time when the two of you will really need that money. Don't you think it's enough if you see each other every three months? Just think how hard you have to work for your money, and how quickly you could spend it all in London! Am I right or am I right?

It's possible that I might extend my stay here by a week. I haven't really been able to relax at all because of Aunt Bertha's rather serious illness, and I very much wanted to go home in better condition. I've written to Papa, under quite a lot of pressure from everyone here, and asked him whether he would mind terribly if I stayed on a bit, and now I'm waiting to see what he has to say. So keep on writing to Düsseldorf, as usual. Papa will send on the post if I'm still here. He asked me to let you know that he didn't write to you this week because he had to go to Elberfeld just after your letter arrived, and he wanted to send it straight on to me. This time my letter will just have to suffice.

I send you a big big hug, from Papa too,
love Mama

15 February 1938
Düsseldorf

PARENTS TO EDITH

Dear Edith,

Thank you for your lovely letter. I immediately sent it off to Mama, together with the one for Uncle Richard and Aunt Mathilde. I was so glad to hear all your news, but I do think it would be preferable if you went to Cambridge for Easter instead. – I am sure you would be able to make some contacts there which would doubtless be useful to you in the future. If you decline the offer now, you probably won't be invited again. Can you not afford the fare? Lore Herz left for England again yesterday. She'll be bringing along your red dress; I also gave her your address. She won't be able to send the dress to you because for various reasons she is completely broke at the moment. She'll send you a note, and you'll have to decide between you how best to sort out the conveyance. Maybe you could send her some German Marks for the postage? I do wish you would write a little more clearly. There were various parts of your letter which I couldn't decipher at all.

Warm kisses,
Papa

My dear girl,

I'm afraid you're going to have to be satisfied with this short letter for today. Papa's contribution has only just arrived here, and I'm about to leave for Göttingen as Uncle Alfred was operated on yesterday. Do send him a little note when you have the chance. Wolfgang complains that you never write to him. I quite agree with Papa about your visit to Cambridge. If there's any way you can do it, I really think you should. What is the Inter-Aid club? Why doesn't Wolfgang want to join it? I'll write about everything else next week, or maybe from Göttingen.

A thousand kisses from Mama

1 March 1938
Düsseldorf

FRIEDA TO EDITH

My dearest girl,

You mustn't be angry with Eva-Maria for not writing regularly; she really is in a most unenviable situation. She works in the office all day, goes twice a day to the clinic, and has to fit all sorts of other little jobs in between. We hope with all our hearts that Uncle Alfred will soon be released from his pain – he is suffering so much. And Eva-Maria will only be able to settle down herself when all this is over. Nobody imagined that things would turn out so differently, and so quickly too! Did I ask you already not to tell Uncle Richard about the gravity of the situation? He will find out soon enough, and he always seems so affected by these things. The future now looks a little more problematic; it's unlikely that Eva-Maria will be able to find a job here. I wish we could talk about all this as a family – I find it so exhausting to discuss everything in writing! You write that you find it hard to imagine what we're up to these days, but I'm sure that's not true. I always try to tell you anything that's worth knowing, as far as my time allows.

So you think I should have a rest after my 'relaxing holiday'. Yes, my child, if only that were possible! I was so looking forward to Sunday, when I planned to really put my feet up. The telephone rang at seven in the morning. Of course my first thought was Göttingen, but the person on the other end said they were calling on behalf of Frau Heinic, and that I should get to the hospital as soon as I could. I pulled on my clothes and raced to the hospital to find that Herr Heinic had just died. They'd operated and everything was fine, but then his heart gave out. I took her home with me, and Paul too (Alfred is of course in Paris), and we kept them here with us for the first night. I've got a week's pass to travel to Mönchengladbach, and I go and see her as often as I can. We're going to the funeral together tomorrow. Will you write to her? I feel so sorry for her, and she has nobody she's really close to here. – So you can see that my idea of taking it easy has completely failed. On top of that I'm waiting to be summoned to Göttingen any moment, and my bags are packed.

I hope you spent a lovely day with Fräulein Grete on Sunday, and I'm sure the first day at school was wonderful. There must have been so much going on! Should I visit Frau Kleinertz before she leaves, and give her something little to take along for you? I envy her and I'd desperately like to be going myself. – Don't forget that Herbert Hamacher is to be confirmed on 13 March, and that it's Aunt Hanni's birthday on the 18th and Aunt Mathilde's on the 24th, and Grandma will be eighty on 3 April. Please make a note of all this. I don't know whether I'll think of reminding you again. – That's all for today!

Warmest kisses from Mama

2 March 1938
Düsseldorf

GEORG TO EDITH
Dear Mouse,

I think it's difficult to predict with any certainty how things will develop in Göttingen, but I do believe it may still be some weeks until the end. I know the situation can't be easy for Eva-Maria, with all those extra tasks, and it's made even less easy by the fact that we can only rarely support her from here with snippets of advice in isolated cases. It seems to me from your letters that, all difficulties aside, you are really enjoying your work and training. That makes me so happy. I can't tell you much about what I'm doing, only that I will be able to do my own work again soon.* Of course that's what matters to me more than anything. Recently I saw my name quoted again in a piece in a German academic journal.

With loving kisses,
Papa

---

* This may be an oblique reference to the fact that Georg Lindemeyer had to undertake a period of forced labour.

9 March 1938
Göttingen

EVA-MARIA AND FRIEDA TO EDITH

My dear Edith,

You're furious with me, I know, but I hope you won't be any longer when you understand why I couldn't write. Uncle Alfred passed away on Thursday 3 March. He was operated on, and spent the next fifteen days at the clinic in the most dreadful pain. Mama has been here since Thursday evening, and Papa arrives on Saturday night, because now of course we need a lawyer. Aunt Bertha was here, but she left again this morning. Uncle Richard is here too and will be staying until Sunday. The funeral is on Sunday, and we're going to Kassel on Monday for the cremation. – These last few weeks have been so terrible and chaotic that I simply couldn't write. But thankfully he was not aware of his death, and was asleep for the last two days. He was completely confused for the whole of the final week; you really couldn't get any sense out of him at all. In fact his death was a release for him. Now it's come to pass that the house belongs to me. I'll write to you about everything else soon. At the moment I'm only going into the office in the mornings, and on 1 April I'm stopping for good. I wonder whether we'll be able to see each other soon? As soon as everything is over, when everybody has left again, I'll write to you at greater length.

                    Millions of kisses from Eva-Maria

My dearest girl,

Eva-Maria has told you the most important things, and I can't write much today; I'm upset and rather overwhelmed.

I'm trying to get Eva-Maria over to England for eight or ten days in April. She is in urgent need of a rest, and her passport is still valid until 10 May. Aunt Bertha is going to try to arrange for her to stay with relatives in London, unless you know of anyone else. I'll write more about everything next week. Unfortunately I won't be able to visit Frau Kleinertz as I'll hardly be back before 1 April. I'll send chocolate and the hat. That's all for now.

A thousand kisses from Mama

22 March 1938
Göttingen

FRIEDA TO EDITH
My dear child,

I'm sending you this extra letter as I want you to post the enclosed reply coupon to Frau Bondi yourself. I think that would only be right, and please do it soon. I hope to be able to send you ten Marks shortly. Papa wrote to the tax office today to enquire about it. It's much better to have everything in order, and as soon as we have the go-ahead from them we can send you the money regularly. I'm going to have to be very brief today as I've got so much work to get on with. As soon as I have a bit of peace and quiet back in Düsseldorf, I'll be able to catch up on everything and write longer letters. We could really use you here – there's so much to do.

A thousand kisses,
Mama

At the end of April Eva-Maria travelled to England for two weeks to visit Edith and Wolfgang, and to meet Wolfgang's teachers.

27 April 1938
Düsseldorf

FRIEDA TO EDITH AND EVA-MARIA

My dear girls,

Today it's my little Edith's nineteenth birthday, and my thoughts have been with and around you since early this morning! I kept closing my eyes and imagining that any moment the birthday girl would creep into my bed, demanding to be congratulated! Late yesterday evening we heard a simply wonderful broadcast of 'Carmen' from the Rome opera house. A worthy beginning to 27 April!

We can see from your letter, dear eldest daughter, that you've already done all kinds of fabulous things over there, and that you're having a lovely time. Has the weather cheered up since? It's absolutely lovely here today, so beautiful in fact that the general consensus of one person (Papa) is that we'll celebrate the birthday by going for a walk. I'm delighted that your day trip with Fräulein Grete went so well, and I'm sure that's the best way to learn about the country properly. It's rather splendid, the way they look after you, and I'm just about to write to her to say so. I can well imagine that you find them extremely encouraging, and they are probably right: we should only be taking into account what's best for you, and not think about ourselves at all. There is simply too much at stake. By human estimations you still have a long life ahead of you, so we, and you too, shouldn't be planning things in terms of what suits us all best at the moment. We have no right to, but more importantly we have a Christian duty to think further ahead, into the future. Please consider all this and talk it all through thoroughly with Edith; you can also discuss the pros and cons with Fräulein Grete. – When are you thinking of coming back? For various reasons I'd like to know as soon as possible what time you'd be getting to Gladbach or Düsseldorf.

More than anything I'd like to hear all about your time with Wolfgang. The letter I got from him yesterday was again very uninformative. He didn't write a single word acknowledging the serious tone of my last letter, and I'm so worried about him, really afraid sometimes. None of you should ever keep anything from me; I am always able to tell how you really are. I hope the rest of the days you have together are sunny, and I send you both many fat kisses,

Your Mama

1 May 1938
Düsseldorf

PARENTS TO EDITH AND EVA-MARIA
My dear girls,

Your first week together is over, and I expect that Eva-Maria will be back here next Sunday evening, 8 May. But please write and tell me exactly when you'll be coming, and whether you'll be changing in Gladbach. I'm always so thrilled to hear that Edith is enjoying her work and seems so contented.

So yesterday you were together with Wolfgang. You know you'll still have to go to Brackley, whatever happens – it's extremely important to me that you do. If it really is the case that he's further ahead than his fellows, that should be an incentive for him to try to move up two years and get to another level – there's no reason why that should not be possible. I'll sit tight and see what you have to say about it all. Tomorrow I'll be sending off the ten Marks for May, and I hope it will arrive punctually.

That's all for today. In eight days from now, you'll be telling me so much about your trip that my ears will be ringing.

Big cuddles to both of you from Mama

My dear children,

There's not much to report from here, and anything there is to say Mama has said already. I'm also keen to hear all about your weekend. Fortunately I am able to do at least a bit of my own work again, alongside the various bits and pieces to do with Uncle Alfred's estate. Dienstag wrote to tell me that he couldn't print my piece in the latest issue because too much material has already been submitted from abroad; he said he'd probably publish it in the next one – it's been typeset and I've already read the proofs. I hope you have many more wonderful days together.

Warmest kisses,
your Papa

15 May 1938
Düsseldorf

PARENTS TO EDITH

My dear child,

Your letter of today gave us much joy, as it proves again just how well you're getting on over there; the whole tone of it is happy, and of course that remains the most important thing! From all the descriptions Eva-Maria has given me, I now have a clear image of your surroundings and all your friends. I wonder whether I will ever have the opportunity to get to know everything there myself?! Please write to Grandma as soon as possible to thank her for the piece of needlework. I went to see her yesterday, and she still didn't know if her parcel had arrived.

Would you mind very much going to see Miss d'Avigdor to discuss the following with her: what sort of vocational training possibilities would Wolfgang have if he stayed on to take the Matura exams (which surely wouldn't be before 1941), and what would happen if he left school now and had some technical training instead? Would he be able to get anywhere without a school-leaving certificate, or would that be a permanent handicap for him? Mr Bolton has written to ask what we think might be best. He would incline more towards a technical training for Wolfgang, as Inter-Aid would hardly support him (nor can it) if he only takes his Matura when he's eighteen. We want to have a good think about all this in the holidays, and weigh everything up, but it's so much more difficult to make judgements about these things from a distance. At least you could determine everything that needs to be brought into the equation. If you could call on Inter-Aid personally, it would be much easier than asking all those questions in writing from here: first of all you can't continually pester people for answers, and secondly you get much more from a face-to-face conversation. There's no great hurry, so you can go whenever it suits you best.

A big fat kiss from Mama

Dear Edith,

We're always so glad about the cheerful tone of your letters, and Eva-Maria's descriptions confirm that you tackle your considerable workload happily and with confidence. As you know we've now had more appreciative news about Wolfgang from Mr Bolton; it seems as though he's taken our admonishments to heart. At the moment the thing that gives us the greatest joy here is our new radio set, which you will soon become acquainted with yourself.

Loving kisses,
Papa

22 May 1938
Düsseldorf

FRIEDA AND EVA-MARIA TO EDITH

My dear child Edith,

On which date do your holidays begin? Do you think you'll be able to travel with Wolfgang? I can scarcely wait, and I become quite high-spirited when I think that it might really be possible for all five of us to spend four weeks together, and to see and talk to each other constantly. Write and let me know the date as soon as you can; then it will seem all the more tangible! When you write next, we'll be sitting here with Aunt Bertha and Uncle Josi – they're coming on Thursday and staying through Whitsun. We're so looking forward to it, but it would be lovelier still if you could all be here too! And then on the 8th we're planning to set off for the Black Forest for three weeks; Dr Bergenthal thinks it would be the best thing for me, and I think it will also do Papa and Eva-Maria the world of good. It's much cheaper in the early part of the season, so that's when we're planning to go.

We're glad that you'll be going to see Miss d'Avigdor that day. It's simply impossible to judge everything from here, and yet we're desperate to gather as much information as we can about all these issues – it's so important for the boy's future. I received such a lovely letter from Mr Freer telling me how much he enjoyed having Wolfgang to stay. It does me the world of good when I hear things like that. – Tomorrow Frau Kleinertz and her daughter are coming to visit, but unfortunately Eva-Maria won't be here: she has a temporary job until 1 June and has to work all day. She's delighted to be earning a little, but I always look forward to the evenings, when she comes home.

A thousand kisses,
Mama

Dear Fatty!

I'm awfully excited about the Black Forest. I hope the weather will be halfway decent. By the way, have you had any news about my airmail letter since? – How lovely that you're getting the chance to play a bit of tennis. It's a terrible shame that I won't be here when Ilse Kleinertz comes to visit, but of course I'm very glad to have this extra work.

Please send my best regards to everyone who deserves them!

Infinite kisses from Eva-Maria

7 June 1938
Düsseldorf

PARENTS TO EDITH

My dear girl,

Today I have time to write you only a very short note. Aunt Bertha and Uncle Josi are leaving the day after tomorrow, and we're setting off on Friday, so you can imagine all the work I have to get done between now and then. I promise to send you a long letter from Friedenweiler, and I'll tell you everything that's been going on here over the past few days. – If you get this letter before you go to see Miss d'Avigdor, it might be a good idea if you could raise the issue of Wolfgang's confirmation again. It's impossible to tell what will happen here this year, but I'm sure the local confirmation dates won't coincide with English school holidays. He is getting so big that the whole business is now rather pressing and simply can't be put off any longer, so I need to know for what length of time he has to be registered there in order to be confirmed at the earliest possible opportunity, and what that next date is. But the most important thing for you to discuss is his career, which you should explore in as much depth as possible so that we can form a clear picture of it all. Please send your next letter to 'Friedenweiler, bei Neustadt im Schwarzwald, Pension Waldesruh'.

I'm sure the time between now and 30 July will pass incredibly quickly – I can hardly wait! This time it will be quite an occasion!

A thousand and one fat kisses (plus one from me = 1002, Aunt Bertha),

Mama

Dear child,

I'm in a great hurry today, so I can only send you a very short greeting. By the way, are you still in contact with the people in Haslemere? I'd like to know because of the manuscripts I sent to Fräulein Wolf when you were there.

Warmest kisses,

Papa

13 June 1938
Friedenweiler, bei Neustadt im Schwarzwald

FRIEDA TO EDITH

My dear girl,

Your lovely letter arrived this morning, delayed by a day. But up here that's not entirely surprising; the people behave as if they have all the time in the world, and they're certainly never in a hurry. Unfortunately we've been terribly unlucky with the weather. It's been raining and blowing since we arrived on Saturday evening. Papa and Eva-Maria have gone on many walks in the beautiful woods around here, but that kind of exercise is no good for me; there's so much climbing and my heart simply doesn't behave itself. So instead I just lie around in the room and don't get anything out of being here at all. Eva-Maria has just discovered somewhere nearby where you can hire a sun-lounger for the day for only 30 Pfennig. If nothing else comes up, I think I'll go along and do that from tomorrow. Our trip was wonderful, and it only rained briefly once. We left at eight on Friday morning and got to Heidelberg at around two. We only got up to the castle in the afternoon, and later we went on to Neckarstein, a quite delightful, beautiful old town on the River Neckar. On Saturday morning Papa and Eva-Maria went off for a walk, very admirably, and I stayed behind in the hotel. Then we set off again at around two in the afternoon, and arrived here at seven after an extraordinarily beautiful drive through the Höllental. I have to say it's very picturesque here. But if the weather goes on like this, it's not going to be much fun for me.

It's quite exasperating that you didn't get to speak to Miss d'Avigdor. When do you think you might now be able to do that? It won't be possible to get Wolfgang confirmed here on Palm Sunday next year, because it falls on 2 April. In Germany the last confirmations have to take place before April, because on that day a whole lot of school leavers go off to start their land year,* or to begin other jobs. You'll have to decide how best to arrange it. I simply can't assess

* Voluntary service in agriculture.

that from here, but it may be that we'll have to correspond with Mr Bolton about it. You wanted to know what's wrong with Fräulein Poensgen. I think she has some kind of stomach complaint which seems to be causing her a great deal of trouble. Do write to her soon – she'd like that. She always writes me such lovely letters. – The two weeks we had with Aunt Bertha and Uncle Josi were very nice indeed. They're always so jolly, and we spent a lovely few days together. We went to Drachenfels for the day on Whit Sunday, and on the 2nd to Kalkum-Angermund. We also managed to fit in excursions to Kaiserswerth, Münchenwerth and Zons, but Papa and I didn't go with them to Schloss Bing. – The holidays are really not too far off at all now. Only forty-eight days until 30 July! I only hope nothing gets in the way of your trip.

A thousand loving kisses from your Mama

22 June 1938
Friedenweiler, bei Neustadt im Schwarzwald
FRIEDA TO EDITH
My dear girl,

We haven't heard from you at all this week! We'll hope for something on Friday – I so miss your letters when they don't come. I can't have you here with me for my birthday on Friday, so I've sent three pictures of us over to you instead. I hope my parcel got to you on time. Since I can't do any baking here, I'm going to have to delay the usual shipment of a sample of birthday cake, and do it for you later.

We're probably going to stay on here until Monday 4 July, and we'll get home on the 5th. Then it's only twenty-two days until Wolfgang comes home, and three days later we'll finally have the full complement again! I only hope everything works out! Just think, Wolfgang hasn't even been issued with his passport yet, and I'm already anxious that he might not get it in time. Do you think you could look into it again, just once more?

Here the weather has finally cheered up. It's wonderfully warm, and if it stays like this the three of us will come home looking like negroes. And soon we'll be able to tell you all about our trip in person. It's really rather beautiful here, a lovely part of the world. I've found a wonderful little spot for my deckchair, and that's what I love best of all. Sometimes I sit back and doze in it for hours, or I'll read a bit, but only rarely. My favourite thing is just to look out on to the huge black fir trees all around the meadow where I'm sitting. – So, my girl, think of me a little on Friday.

A huge hug and a kiss from your Mama

25 June 1938
Friedenweiler

GEORG TO EDITH
Dear Edith,

I've got a quiet half-hour, so I thought I'd write to you. It's hard to say whether your application will be successful. These things are always down to luck. The main reasons for applying are the necessity of dental treatment and to get some new clothes. I can't really give you any sound advice as I don't know what the most important requirements are, nor can I find them out, and I know just as little about circumstances over there. The best would be if Ellen could try to find someone who has a contact at the authority that makes the ultimate decision, and then to take along a written opinion from a dentist on the necessity of having the treatment. Then you could also explain your need for clothes to them in person. We wouldn't have been able to speak on the phone – we'd probably never have got through to each other. There must be three or four telephone exchanges between here and London, so the call would only have got to you at around midnight, if at all, and I doubt either of us would have been able to understand a word the other was saying. Now, 'perforce', I must close!

Loving kisses from Papa

7 July 1938
Düsseldorf

FRIEDA AND EVA-MARIA TO EDITH

You poor old thing!

I feel so, so sorry for you, and I'm keeping my fingers permanently crossed for the pain to have gone away by now. I do hope that you don't have to suffer too much during your holidays. I assume from your card that you've been to see a dentist. Who will be paying for that? I've just paid in your money at the post office, but it certainly won't be enough for a dentist! – We got home late last night, and Eva-Maria is most put out that our lovely holiday had to come to an end. It was simply wonderful, even though the sun wasn't always shining, and I hope that the benefits we gained from it will be long lasting.

This letter will have to be short, but we'll be able to chat about everything when you're home. Only three weeks to go!

Warm kisses, and all the very, very best for a speedy recovery!

Mama

My dear Edith,

Have you still got a toothache? I hope it's not as bad as it was. Here's some news: Hilde is going over to England for two months in August and September, spending six weeks in Darlington in the north, and a few days in London at the end. Isn't that fantastic? On Monday I'm going to start working half-days again, this time at the Mendel & Neuberger offices, and for the other half of the day I'll be taking language lessons. I think first English then French and then Spanish would be the right way to do it. Hilde is so looking forward to England and to seeing you again, unless you have to be here just at that time for your silly old toothache. Get better soon and give my best regards to anyone who wants them.

Lots and lots of big fat kisses from Eva

10 July 1938
Düsseldorf

PARENTS TO EDITH

My dear girl,

Our letters must have crossed, and you should have got ours too by now. We sent it off a little later than normal because of our return journey, but please don't tell me that it's met the same fate as my birthday letter, which I am still lamenting! I'm a little worried that you've written in pencil. Now, hand on heart, is it really true that you've run out of ink, or was that a white lie and you're in fact ill? It would really be quite wrong to keep anything from me, and it will only end up making me even more worried than I need to be. I'm glad that your teeth are slowly recovering. With any luck that will continue and the pain will go altogether. At least you have lots of other things to distract you: the Speech Day and all its preparations should be cause for plenty of work and excitement. I'm now desperate to know whether you both have your return visas and travel permits! You *absolutely must not* travel without them; it would be far too risky. I wonder, how will everything turn out? Do you think we'll be spending Sunday together in three weeks' time?! You must both write and tell me what you'd like on the menu for your special home-coming supper. Who knows, I may even have a cleaning lady by then!

Unfortunately Frau Hohaus is no longer allowed to work, but I'll do everything I can to find someone so we really enjoy our time together. I hope your teeth get better and better, and keep smiling for the next three weeks.

Lots of kisses from Mama

Dear child,

I so hope that your toothache will soon be gone. It would be preferable if the whole problem could be treated here in Germany.

In haste, with loving kisses,
Papa

20 July 1938
Düsseldorf

GEORG AND EVA-MARIA TO EDITH

Dear Edith,

Today's message upset us both very much, but above all we feel sorry for *you*. You're now so alone in a foreign country, with no one to comfort you. We're sure you'll still get the travel permit, even if it is too late for this trip, and then maybe you could come for Christmas instead. I do believe you have enough reasons to give your application at least a fair chance of success.

I just wanted to say one thing about your 'substitute plan': of course I think the best idea would be for you to go to Paris. I'm sure that would be most useful for you; it would enlarge your range of vision and give you an idea of circumstances in France in comparison with England. But there is this one complication: according to German law, as a German citizen you need to have a particular stamp in your passport to travel to France, and this is probably issued by German consulates abroad. Without this stamp, entry into France is punishable under German law. If you went ahead with the trip without the stamp, and then got an entry stamp in your passport from the French border authorities, no German authority would agree to extend your passport. The consequences of this don't need to be spelled out. So you're either going to have to try to obtain this particular stamp or give up your plan altogether.

Warm kisses,

Papa

Dearest Edith,

Are you absolutely sure that *nothing* can be done? Even if you went there again in person and complained so much that they *had* to do something? You could also say that you've just received your Certificate of Unobjectionability,* and that as far as the German authorities are concerned there's nothing to prevent you from travelling. Otherwise they wouldn't have issued you with the certificate in the first place. You really must keep your chin up. As you said to me yourself once, the most important thing is that you stay in England for the time being, even if it means you can't come home to see us! But do try everything you can, just one more time.

10000 kisses from Eva-Maria

24 July 1938
Düsseldorf

FRIEDA TO EDITH
My dear Edith,

Your letter has just arrived here, and I see from it that you are gradually coming to terms with what cannot be avoided, and looking forward to your trip to Paris. Well, it does seem to be the best solution and I hope with all my

---

* In order to leave the German Reich legally, Jewish people needed the so-called 'Unbedenklichkeitsbescheinigung' (Certificate of Unobjectionability): this was only issued on proof of having paid all outstanding taxes and fees, from actual or fictitious tax arrears through the discriminatory charges imposed on Jews, such as the Reich Flight Tax and the Jewish property tax, to allegedly unpaid telephone bills and the like. Further, would-be emigrants had to sign a 'voluntary' waiver of all their property.

heart that you will have a wonderful stay there, and above all that you'll have some peace and quiet, and time to relax. Are you going to have all your post forwarded? *Maybe* while you're there you'll get your travel permit, and then there might be a bit of time left for you to come and see us. That would be so wonderful that I hardly dare to imagine it! Of course you know that you can turn up here unannounced at any time of the day or night, if ever there's the opportunity. I'm sure Hilde will be able to bring you the things you need if you tell us where she can leave them for you. She won't be travelling until early August, so do write soon and tell us precisely what you want, with *detailed* instructions. I'm sure you'll have got the cake by now. It's a slice of what was to be your home-coming cake, which now you'll have to eat there. I baked it in our new Kitchen Wonder. – It now seems certain that Wolfgang will be able to come over. The boy will be so thrilled! If only I knew that you weren't so sad any more, and that you're now looking forward to Paris, then I'd promise not to mention it again. Do you think you'll be leaving on Saturday? I hope you have a truly wonderful trip, a good rest and a wonderful holiday.

Warmest kisses,
Mama

Edith did not in fact travel to Paris in August 1938. Instead, the necessary permit arrived on time, and she was able to go home to the family in Düsseldorf, where Wolfgang was also spending his holidays.

31 August 1938
Düsseldorf

GEORG TO EDITH

Dear child,

We were so happy to get your card, delayed though it was, and to read that you'd arrived back in England safely. So in the end your trip was a happy one, despite the fact that it was in some respects beset with so much worry and uncertainty. Even though it was a particularly chaotic time, you came home for three whole weeks, and that's not something everyone can do. We all have reason to be thankful for that. I hope all is going well in Broadstairs, and particularly that the weather is good.

When I had my consultation with the people at the passport office, I discovered that I might be able to get a passport after all. But it's still not clear whether I'd be able to travel with Wolfgang. All the best, my dear child, and write soon.

Warmest kisses,
Papa

31 August 1938
Düsseldorf

WOLFGANG TO EDITH

Dear Edith,

So you've arrived at last! Mama had already got herself into quite a state because you wrote so late.

I hope you've been having some decent weather at the seaside. Here the weather is absolutely awful. Yesterday we wanted to go to the fair at Neuss, but it rained so much that we went to the cinema instead. Mama and Eva-Maria went to see the Benjamino Gigli film 'Die Stimme des Herzens', and I went to 'Krach und Glück um Künnemann'. Both films were a complete load of rubbish. Papa went to the library.

I've now got a couple of insoles for my flat feet, but they're dreadfully uncomfortable. I'm awfully lazy about writing, which is why I'm using this typewriter – – –

1000000000000000000000000000000000000000000000-00000 kisses,

Wolfgang

4 September 1938
Düsseldorf

FRIEDA TO EDITH

My dear girl,

Your first letter finally arrived today. It sounds as though you've got a huge amount to do, and I hope you don't find your work too exhausting. I'm sure you will do it so well that everyone will be thrilled with you. Is the weather quite nice there now? That's the main thing when you're by the sea. It's awful that you were in such a mad rush when you got to London. The Ellens were sweet to have looked after you so well. They also wrote us a very nice letter, but there wasn't a single word from them or from you about our plans, so I shall just assume that you all think they're hopeless!

Yesterday Papa received written confirmation from Mr Bolton, so it might now be possible for him to go over to England for a few days. Please send us a card *by return* to let us know when you'll be back in Chislehurst. It would be best if Papa and Wolfgang could travel on the 18th, but there would be little point if you're still in Broadstairs – it would be much better if you could be there with them at the Inter-Aid meeting. I can also write to Inter-Aid and ask whether they can accommodate Wolfgang for the night of the 18th, but I'll only do that when I have your answer. I'll also ask Miss d'Avigdor whether it would be possible to find somewhere for Papa to stay so that he could get by very simply for a few days on his ten Marks. The main thing is that Wolfgang's various career alternatives will be discussed during that meeting. He'll be leaving us again in two weeks. That's all for today.

A thousand kisses,
Mama

PS Did you get the money I sent off on 30 August?

The concern expressed in the following letters refers to the imminent threat of war. It was averted at the Munich Conference on 29 September 1938, when Britain and France acquiesced in Nazi Germany's annexation of the Sudetenland.

26 September 1938
Düsseldorf

FRIEDA TO EDITH
My dear child,

Your card has just arrived. Papa's arrangements are not yet fixed, but of course we'll send you a card by airmail as soon as we know anything for certain. Of course everything is so insecure at the moment that it's hard to plan for even an hour ahead. Do you really believe that we don't know how things might turn out if you stay there? Despite all this careful consideration (or perhaps because of it) we decided to leave you there, but only after we'd talked to people in similar circumstances. Whatever happens, it's the best thing for you. Besides, it would be impossible for you to travel without a permit, and you certainly wouldn't get one at such short notice. Quite apart from anything else, you have to think that you'd be putting your entire future at stake if you left now – even for a short time (which you of all people shouldn't even contemplate) – whereas if you stayed you would be able to keep your options open. What is Brigitte going to do, and what about the others you know?

Let's all just hope that the worst can be averted, and that this won't go to the last extreme. But if the situation does change, we'll also have to keep our heads low and accept things as they come. We cannot possibly struggle with Fate. We can only do what we can to keep ourselves going for each other, and to hope for a time when we will be together again. Our dear God has not abandoned us in difficult times in the past, so why should we suddenly forget that he is protecting us even now? Keep thinking of that, my dear child, and never abandon hope: one day everything will change! Until now you've always been the one we've turned our eyes to, and you have to remain that person.

I'm writing today because I don't know if it will still be possible tomorrow. This evening we'll know more. By the time you get this letter I'm sure everything will have been decided. Whatever happens, you know that I have no other thoughts but of you, my children, and that I am with you always, with every one of my senses. I hope to hear from you soon that everything has settled down.

Big hugs and kisses, my dear girl,
from your Mama

PS I'm sure you don't need to worry about Wolfgang. Remember that he's now *fifteen years old*!

28 September 1938
Düsseldorf

PARENTS AND EVA-MARIA TO EDITH

My dear child,

I'm writing today so that you have some kind of sign of life from us again. This morning I spoke with a whole lot of people whose children are in the same situation as you, and they all seem to be of the same opinion. Everyone is glad that their children are in England, despite the risk that there may come a time when it's no longer possible to keep in touch with them. We are acutely aware of how hard this will be for us, and for the other parents too, but to do anything else would be sheer madness. Of course we're all still hoping that the danger will pass, and that the world will recognise that to go to war would be insanity! Even now it's impossible to say whether or not that hope will be fulfilled, but until war becomes an incontrovertible certainty I simply cannot believe in it.

I do hope you haven't got Wolfgang too worked up about all this. The boy must stay where he is, and if he doesn't he will be nothing in life. What would happen if he came back here? He wouldn't get into school any more, and a private tutor at home is out of the question, so what could he do? I hope with all my heart that when you've considered everything thoroughly you will not only understand our point of view but also find it completely justified. I'm sure you know how happy I would be if I could have you all around me again, but I am not so selfish that I would want this at the cost of your well-being! Yesterday evening we heard Chamberlain talking and we were surprised to hear how pleasant and calm the old man sounds!

I hope that very soon I'll receive a letter from you which is calm and reflective, and which shows me that you understand us! Day and night we've been weighing up all the pros and cons, and looking at the situation from all angles, but we cannot arrive at a different conclusion.

I send you a huge kiss and hold you very close to my heart,

Mama

Dear Edith,

Unfortunately I wasn't at home when you telephoned yesterday evening. Dear old thing, you mustn't get yourself into such a panic!! Here we're constantly listening to the radio and all the various news reports, and I can assure you we're very much in the picture! And anyway, you're not the only people in England with parents who are still in Germany. We really can judge the situation quite well. You simply *mustn't* always get Mama into such a state and confuse her like this. I've told you this before, you just can't do that any more. I entirely understand your position, but you shouldn't let yourself be unsettled so easily – everything will happen in its own time. Instead of instantly losing your head, what about thinking things through sensibly first and then deciding what's best!

Mama hasn't read what I've written here. Anyway, I know you won't be angry with me for telling you exactly what I think. I'm only thinking about you, after all, so come on, chin up and chest out!

A thousand hugs from your Eva-Maria

Dear Edith,

None of the Düsseldorf children who are over in England are coming back. We have to remain calm, monitor the developments, and let things run their course. Try to be brave and have a little self-control!

Loving kisses from Papa

10 October 1938
Düsseldorf

PARENTS TO EDITH

My dear girl,

I cannot express quite how elated we are that the great danger hanging over us has now been averted, at least for the time being. Now that you're back in Chislehurst I'll send your money off this afternoon.

Papa has received a letter from Mr Bolton asking him to come up to the school for a meeting. We aren't yet sure what he will do, but we should definitely know by the end of the week. Now they're telling us that he needs another document to say that he has somewhere to stay, and that he'll be able to get by on the ten-Mark allowance because he's being looked after and so on. If you could get hold of something like that for him, then please do so *immediately*. Otherwise he'll just try and go without it, but it's rather doubtful whether that will work.

Did you tell Miss d'Avigdor that Papa has written to her to ask whether she could arrange some cheap accommodation for him? He wants to know whether he should write again to say that he's coming, and refer to his previous, still unanswered letter. *On no account* should it seem as though he wants something from her. You will have time to write her a short card on the matter, won't you? There's really not much news to send you from here. On Saturday I went to see Grandma, who sends you her best wishes. It's amazing how sprightly she still is, even though she's already eighty.

I think it quite splendid of Frau Schlossmann that she wrote to you. It makes me happy to know that if there was an emergency over there, you wouldn't feel completely isolated. Did you write back to her?

> Keep well, my dear girl, lots of warm kisses
>
> from Mama

Dear child,

It's very reassuring to know that you're back in Chislehurst, not least for my own sake. Things would otherwise have been even more difficult for me if I actually make it over to England. It is extremely urgent that you write to Miss d'Avigdor, as Mama has asked you to, because as soon as she's received your card I'll be able to write to her again myself.

Warm kisses,
Papa

18 October 1938
Düsseldorf

PARENTS AND EVA-MARIA TO EDITH
Dearest child,

I'm afraid I have some very sad news for you: yesterday evening Leo called to say that Aunt Hanni had died. I'm sure you can understand that I don't feel like writing much today. I'm still so haunted by this dreadful news that I simply cannot think of anything else. She had pyelitis, an inflammation of the kidney, and in the course of this she also developed a mania. I think you know what that means; you've had all kinds of experience in that area.

By the way, your last letter and Wolfgang's were opened by customs. But since we all have good consciences and have done nothing and written nothing wrong, it doesn't really matter. I'll write more next time.

Warmest kisses from Mama

Dear Edith,

I know you too will be extremely shocked by Mama's news. What will become of all these men living on their own? I heard this morning that I've been issued with a Certificate of Unobjectionability for my financial status, which I've been chasing after for weeks. I think it's now likely that I will also get a passport, and I hope that means I'll then be issued with a visa for England. I'm sure the whole thing will still drag on for a few more days. If I write to Miss Giles from here, do I have to tell her exactly when I'm going to be visiting? I don't think I can be that precise about the dates yet – I'll only know them when I'm in London and I'm able to organise my time over there properly.

Loving kisses,
Papa

Dear little Edith,

Here's a very short but sweet note with a kiss from me, because I've got English soon and I've still got to prepare for it. Hilde and Ruth always come over on Mondays now, and we speak English together and read little extracts from Katherine Mansfield. It's all great fun. More next time.

1000000 warm kisses,
Eva-Maria

31 October 1938
London

GEORG TO EDITH

Dear child,

I was so glad to hear your voice once more. I couldn't

speak longer because the hotel management wouldn't allow it. When I went to the Internationale judenchristliche Allianz [International Jewish-Christian Alliance] I discovered the following:

1. The Alliance's negotiations concerning emigration are still in their initial stages, and this also applies to emigration to Cyprus. So their success in this area cannot yet be determined, and whatever information Weisenstein has to the contrary is wrong.

2. If Eva-Maria comes over here to work as a teacher, her permit will only be valid *for that particular profession*, so she cannot then go on to do an office job. For that she would need another permit, and this would be issued only after a much longer period. She should spend more time applying from Germany for the administrative jobs that are advertised in the newspapers (*Times*, *Daily Telegraph*). I'm sure she would get one, as language skills are highly sought after. Whichever company employs her would then have to arrange for a permit and visa on her behalf.

I got this last bit of information from Fräulein Gretzel at the Internationale judenchristliche Allianz. She is a young Austrian of your age who is employed there as an interpreter. *You must see to it that Lewin checks that all this information is correct.* I can only send you fourteen or fifteen shillings, as I've had to spend far too much on fares, etc. This is another reason why I can't prolong my stay. I enclose money for stamps.

Kisses from Papa

3 November 1938
Düsseldorf

PARENTS TO EDITH

Dear Mouse,

I got back here safe and sound yesterday evening. I am immeasurably happy to have been able to see you and Wolfgang, and to get to know your residences, if only superficially. In Wolfgang's case the impression I got was in every respect excellent. Right now he is living in an optimum environment for learning. The best elements are always simplicity (which keeps all distractions at a distance, forcing you to concentrate) and strict discipline (which is character-building and prepares you to fend for yourself); the Spartans weren't daft, after all, and they also achieved a thing or two.

I was less impressed by Mr Bolton; he seems to lack the intelligence and tact which is essential for his kind of work. But as I told you on the phone, he was forced to admit that Wolfgang has made progress in *every single* subject, and he told me that he would certainly be prepared to keep him on at the school until July 1939. Wolfgang himself claims that he's now top of the class in everything, and he wants to try to move up into the fourth year at Christmas. It would be wonderful if you could write a few lines to him now and then, to acknowledge his efforts and spur him on; of course you shouldn't make it obvious by writing too often.

You know all too well what worries me about your situation. We are all of the opinion that you should *in no circumstances* stay in the bungalow. Please write back immediately to say whether or not Mama can write to Miss Giles asking for you to be moved. Of course she would phrase it in the most polite terms, and would refer to the communications I have had with her about the state of your health and your overall physical development; we could also make the request more palatable by sending along a few pralines (in recognition of Miss Giles's splendid achievements, and her endeavours on your behalf!).

I also must insist that you start visiting Ellen and Grete again. They both feel rather hurt by the fact that you haven't been to see them for so long. Just remember that they are the only people in England who could *instantly* help you out in an emergency, both you and Wolfgang, and they are both prepared to do so at any time. You are going to have to finance the first visit yourself. When you're there you can hint that it's been rather expensive for you to make the trip. Knowing them, they'll then offer to reimburse you for your travel costs in the future. Spending that kind of money won't make the slightest difference to them, and in the circumstances you shouldn't think twice about accepting their offer. You know how sensitive I am in assessing this kind of thing, and I hope this helps you overcome any kind of opposition you may have. Even if they don't offer money for your trip, I certainly wouldn't hesitate to ask them for it.

England made a profound and powerful impression on me. I managed to escape being seasick on the way home by a (very thin) hair's breadth. Mama has just got another letter from Günther Cöhn; he's been shooting crocodiles again, apparently intent on making these fine animals extinct in South Africa. There's one more thing: I left my cushion and a tie in Arden House (61 Princes Square, Queen's Road Underground), and I've told them that you will collect them at some point; there's no hurry of course, and Wolfgang can bring them over with him when he comes.

Warm kisses,
Papa

My dear child Edith,

Today I'll only add a short greeting to Papa's long letter. – By the way, he's only writing a short thank-you note to Miss Giles, so you'll have to write and tell us whether or not you want either of us to write to her at greater length; we might even say that our doctor thinks it dangerous for you to be living in the bungalow. Papa has told me so much about you both, and I'm so happy that he was able to see you and then describe your lives to me.

There's just one other thing: I haven't sewn up the hem on the blue skirt. I only managed to finish it at two in the morning, and Papa was leaving early that day, so I ran out of time. The gloves with the white bit on top might not fit you very well. You can always send them back – one at a time would be best. The pattern wasn't very good, but I'll be able to alter them a bit.

Only a thousand kisses for today,
Mama

8 November 1938
Düsseldorf

PARENTS TO EDITH

My dearest Edith,

I'm delighted you were able to make yourself look so smart with the dress and jacket. I made the skirt quite small on purpose; that material always stretches a bit after you've worn it. I've just bought some quite soft, thin wool, and I'm knitting some long vests for you, which you must promise to wear at all times. I'll send off the first one as soon as I've finished it, and I'll make enough so that you can put a fresh one on regularly, which you'll have to do because you can't boil them. I just hope you don't get ill. Do you need more woollen blankets?

We have just got a letter from Uncle Leo. I feel so sorry for him, having to deal with the boy and do everything on his own. They've recently employed a woman who is supposed to be keeping the house in order for them. You asked how old Aunt Hanni was: only 48! Aunt Bertha is so worried about Peter again. He's been sent home twice from his camp in the Spreewald. I don't know what his plans are now, but there's a possibility that he might even come here for a while. I'm sure it wouldn't be easy, but who knows, we might be able to get somewhere with him. So, my girl, please be careful not to get ill. I worry about you endlessly.

Kisses from Mama

Dear child,

Today I sent sixteen shillings off to you on my permit. We're not sure what the regulations for sending money will be from now on, so you're going to have to spend it wisely. I spoke to Dr E. about the state of your health: he thinks it's most unlikely that your problem has anything to do with haemorrhaging kidneys. The symptoms for that would be different, and those who suffer from it usually have to stop work and take to their beds. Mama doesn't know I'm writing this, nor does she know about your complaint. Günther C. has stopped shooting crocodiles; he's now after baboons instead.

Warmest kisses,
Papa

On 9 November 1938, 7,000 Jewish homes and shops throughout Germany were destroyed in a pogrom known as Reichskristallnacht, *led by Nazi stormtroopers. The following letters barely refer to these events, except to briefly reassure Edith that Eva-Maria, Frieda and Georg Lindemeyer were personally unscathed by the events of that night. This may have been because the Lindemeyers were afraid of the censors, or because they did not want to burden their children living in England with concern for their well-being.*

15 November 1938
Düsseldorf

FRIEDA TO EDITH

My dear child Edith,

Your letter arrived here today at last, and I was so glad to read that you are well. We're also quite well, and I'm making progress with your first vest. It's not going as quickly as I'd like, but I still hope to be able to send it off to you by the end of the week. The next ones will follow as soon as possible. Shall I also send you a little packet of 'Fewa' detergent? It'd be much better to wash your under-clothes in that. Or do you have something similar over there? We're planning to go to Berlin next week for a few days. Please make sure that your next letter gets here on Sunday, or Monday at the latest, so that we get it before we travel. Sorry this is a little short, I'll write more next time.

Warmest kisses from Mama

24 November 1938
Düsseldorf

PARENTS TO EDITH

My dear girl,

I enclose the address of the lady in Chislehurst. Please get in touch with her as soon as you can, and mention Frau Förster from Duisburg. She's a Quaker and stayed for a time with Frau Förster's parents, so she is indebted to them. It seems that Miss Cardwell has moved out, but apparently she lives very close to her old address, which I've given you. You'll be able to get hold of her new address there in any case. It would be best if she could find something for Eva-Maria first. There's not such an urgency for us, because we can always come over later. It's very uncertain when or even whether Hilde will be going over, so we don't want to wait around for that, especially if there's a chance that you might be able to do something beforehand. I'm sorry to be burdening you with all these tasks when you're already working so hard, but in the end it's only for the good of us all, and I hope very much that you'll be able to find the time.

You'll no doubt have received the second vest by now. A third will follow sometime this week. It's essential that you wear them at night too, and I'll try to knit you six altogether so you can change them frequently.

Many kisses from your Mama

My dear little thing,

I'm only going to add a few lines as I'm in the middle of working on a manuscript. My work is progressing well. I'd love to get copies of the special printing of my treatise so that I can send you one, but unfortunately here, as in everything else, the publisher is displaying a slovenliness which verges on the pathological. It's raining and blowing outside. This evening I'm going to the Glücksmanns', as I do every Thursday, to read some of my manuscript to the Professor. All the best for your daily, hard-working existence!

Warmest kisses,
your Papa

30 November 1938
Düsseldorf

PARENTS AND EVA-MARIA TO EDITH

My dear child Edith,

As long as you two are healthy and in good spirits, then we'll both muddle through somehow. It's very sweet of you to get on to the Miss Cardwell thing so quickly – who knows, something may come of her involvement. I'm sure that as Christians we're likely to have our best chance through the Quakers. Guess what happened the night before Advent! Pastor H. sent me a Christmas wreath with a very kind note! We were especially pleased as we hadn't made ourselves one this year. You can rest assured that we're all fine, and that nothing has changed here. I promise you we are, and you just have to believe me! I'm going to finish knitting everything as quickly as I can, and then pack them up and pay duty on them here in advance. Does one also have to pay duty on confectionery, when I send you all those little sweets? We've decided to go and see Aunt Bertha on the 7th, and we're hopeful that we might at least come away from the discussion with something positive. Papa has just composed a long letter to Ellen – we have to try everything we can to achieve something. As soon as we're back from Berlin, Eva-Maria and Papa are both going to start learning bookkeeping as it's done in England. They might have a better chance of getting a job that way, and I could be employed in housekeeping. We're thinking of all kinds of things! It would surely be beneficial if Papa could travel over soon! – Otherwise there's no news from here; I promise you again that we're all fine, as before!

A big, big hug from Mama

PS How are you going to get by with no money at all? We're not permitted to send you the ten Marks any more.* Please let me know you're making ends meet.

---

* After the pogrom it was no longer permitted for Jews to send money abroad.

Dear child,

We were so glad to get your lovely letter after such a long wait, and to hear from you that all is well. Wolfgang made it sound as though your move to that place near Cheltenham was a certainty; then you'd be quite close to each other. I too want to reassure you that *everything* is fine here with us.

Warm kisses,

Papa

Dear Edith,

The parents are cursing me at the moment, saying I'm getting too cheeky. I'm not sure it's true. In the office we're only being employed on a month-by-month basis, as nobody can tell what business will be like in the future. As you may imagine, we've got masses to do just now. Otherwise there's no news. I'm sure I'll write more next time, but now I've run out of space.

Lots of kisses from Eva-Maria

8 December 1938
Berlin

PARENTS AND EVA-MARIA TO EDITH

My dear girl,

We've been in Berlin since yesterday, and already today we made a certain amount of headway. All we can wish for is that we'll be able to go home with a little glimmer of hope. It's a *great* pity that you weren't able to speak to Miss Cardwell. Frau Förster has written to her again since then, so she might have more luck. Hilde has now been given a holiday so she'll be able to travel the moment she gets a convincing invitation and somewhere to live in the city. She wouldn't be able to live too far out as she won't have the money to travel around. – If Eva-Maria's prospective boss wants to keep her here, then of course it would be beneficial if she stayed. I hope very much that I'll soon be able to write to say that an opportunity has come up, after all our efforts.

A thousand kisses,

Mama

PS How fabulous that you bought a camera for Wolfgang!

Loving kisses, Papa

My dear little Edith,

It's great fun in Berlin, and such a shame that you two can't be here with us! We've already seen so much, and our journey was fantastic. More next time – the post-box is just being emptied.

1000 fat kisses,

Eva-Maria

15 December 1938
Berlin

FRIEDA TO EDITH (incomplete)

My poor little Edith,

I'm so sorry to hear that the stupid old frost has caused you so much trouble again. I do hope it'll all clear up soon. Run yourself some warm bubble baths! I put a frost balm into your Christmas package, and you must use it as much as possible. I can always send you another. Hilde was supposed to be travelling to London already this week, but somebody here advised against it, so she's postponed it again. I'd already sent her your Christmas things by express post, and now I've got to write to ask her to send them off to you both from Düsseldorf. I just hope that you'll still get everything on time.

A local priest is going to London in a day or two, and he's said he will try to find something for us when he's there, so Hilde's trip is now less important. I don't have much hope that he'll get anywhere, but we really have to try everything.

Eva-Maria *must* be able to find a position somewhere! There was the possibility that she might work with Miss Eaves in Stoatley Rough, but I can't persuade her to do it as she'd be earning only twelve shillings a week. Also, she'd be so cut off there that she wouldn't have the chance to look for anything else. Please write back *immediately* and let us know what you think. Of course Eva-Maria will also be writing to the employment office, but I'm not promising myself that anything will come of that.

We were so thrilled to get your little photograph. You started at St Mary's exactly a year ago today, so you've only got another year to go! I just wonder whether I'd be able to get a job in housekeeping in England. I would happily do it, just to enable me to come over. But what will Papa do? We are out and about from morning to night, and everybody is so sympathetic to our situation, but there's not yet been any prospect of a solution. Do you think Miss Giles might give you a couple of days off, to try to make some headway on our behalf? We could also write and ask her ourselves. The first thing on your list would be to look up the local priest who's coming over, and ask him to give you some suggestions and a letter of recommendation . . .

20 December 1938
Berlin

PARENTS TO EDITH

My dear, dear Edith,

Christmas has come around again, the second you and Wolfgang will be spending in England! We're going to be thinking of you so much over the feast days, and you can be sure we'll always be in each other's thoughts. Doubtless you'll have seen Hilde by now, and she'll have given you your package. The stockings are from Aunt Bertha, and the rest is from us. We've decided to go back on Thursday, even though we would love to spend Christmas here. But Grandma has just written to say that she wants to come and see us on the 26th, so we'll have to be back home for that. I'm terribly worried about you in all this dreadfully cold weather. Are you still sleeping in the bungalow? It just doesn't bear thinking about. I'll send off some more frost balm to you soon; I've already got some here in fact. Are you otherwise quite healthy? Please promise to tell me the truth! We're sorry to have to leave so soon, but we don't have any choice. Not much good has come of our stay here. Even though we've been on the move constantly, it doesn't appear as though we've made any progress at all. I imagine next Christmas to be quite different, but who can predict the future? We just have to keep on remembering how much and how often we've been helped out in life. We should never forget this, and we must also try to gather the strength to keep on waiting and hoping. My wish is that you spend the holiday happily and healthily. None of us will ever forget how lovely Christmas has been at home in the past.

A big, big hug and an infinite number of kisses

from your Mama

My dear little sister Edith,

It's just so unfair that we can't spend Christmas together. We so wanted to at least spend the two days over Christmas in Berlin, but we can't because of Grandma. And it could have been so much fun!

I wish you and all the other girls a wonderful Christmas; I wonder whether you'll be spending it with Hilde? You two are really going to have to work hard on this thing together. I've run out of time, so I'll write at greater length from Düsseldorf.

100000 Christmas kisses,

your Eva-Maria

I wish you a really healthy, happy Christmas, my dear Edith. We would have liked your dear parents and Eva-Maria to celebrate here with us, but sadly, sadly, it's not to be! Lots of love and a thousand warm greetings from Uncle Josi and Peter, and a fat kiss from your Aunt Bertha.

21 December 1938
Berlin

GEORGE TO EDITH

Dear Mouse,

I have to start by saying that my poor handwriting can be explained by the fact that I'm having to write with a fountain pen, which I don't normally do. I'm sure Mama will have told you already that we're all fine. The two weeks we spent in Berlin were rather exhausting, and so far we haven't seen any actual results. I'm still assuming that something positive can be achieved, however. In my opinion the situation will improve as soon as the two countries concerned have made progress in their negotiations on the question of emigration; at least they have now been initiated. We're heading home tomorrow, and I hope that the train isn't overcrowded. It's been dreadfully cold here for some days now (down to −17°C), with a biting easterly wind. I hope your Christmas presents are delivered to you on time, and that you have a happy Christmas.

Warmest kisses,

Papa

26 December 1938
Düsseldorf

PARENTS AND EVA-MARIA TO EDITH

My dear good Edith,

That really was my favourite Christmas present ever! I just can't tell you how thrilled I was. I'm going to get the big one framed and leave the other one as it is, and put them both up on the wall where Grandma's picture hangs on its own. Then I'll always be able to look at my favourite pictures from where I'm sitting. But I can't stop thinking about the fact that you must have spent every penny you had, and now you'll be even more hard up. You shouldn't really have done it, but I'm still absolutely thrilled that you did!

How wonderful that you were able to spend Christmas with Hilde. So now you know what our situation is. – We were at home alone over Christmas, but Grandma is coming today. Papa's just left to collect her from the station. – Do you know something? I was rather sad to have to do without your Christmas poem for the first time. I always used to love them so, especially as I heard between the lines all kinds of things that you intended especially for me.

I assume that this letter will take rather a long time to get to you this week. In fact I doubt it will be there before New Year, so I'll say now that I hope the year 1939 will fulfil all our dreams, or at least bring us that much closer to their fulfilment! Only a year ago we wouldn't have been able to imagine the drastic changes that have come about in our lives – there was much that was good, but also a great deal that was very sad. But in the New Year we will continue to believe in Him. He has guided us until now and protected us with His hand. Make sure you hold on to your courage and your faith, my dear little girl, and continue to delight us with your strength.

> I send you a big, big hug and a kiss,
> your Mama

Dear Mouse,

Many thanks for the beautiful pictures. We particularly like the large one; I think you look very English in it! But where on earth did you get the money for all these presents? Everything is covered in snow here. A large white blanket is spread out before my window.

Warmest kisses,
Papa

My dear little sister,

Thank you so much for the green cap and the bracelet, which goes together beautifully with my brown necklace. I really wanted one like that but you can't get them here, so I was thrilled. But I like the photograph best of all – I don't think I've ever seen such a fantastic picture.

1000 kisses,
your big sister

Having heard Edith express concern for her sister after Kristallnacht *in November 1938, Mary Cotton, one of Edith's teachers at St Mary's, arranged for her parents to offer a guarantee to employ Eva-Maria as a household help. This was to assist the process of her emigration to England.*

29 December 1938
Düsseldorf

PARENTS AND EVA-MARIA TO EDITH

My dear girl,

You can have no idea how delighted we were to get your letter today. Pray God that it will all become reality, and that we don't get stuck in some impossible situation at the last minute, as so many others have. I will only believe it when the permit is there and we've got through all the complications. It's really quite marvellous that these people who we don't know in the slightest want to give us this wonderful opportunity. It would be particularly beneficial for Eva-Maria to be able to move across before she begins her working life proper, as she'd be able to speak the language constantly in the country itself, and even perfect it. Her English is already rather good, and when we went to the British Consulate in Berlin she spoke nothing but. At the moment in the mornings I'm teaching her to cook, and in the afternoon she has her language lessons, with Spanish too. The main thing is we're now strenuously committed to preparing everything for her departure. Is there anywhere there to store furniture until an apartment has been sorted out? If you can find somewhere, I'll immediately set about getting authorisation to send over the things that you and Eva-Maria were to have when you married.

Of course I am still very willing to take on a job, and I'll do anything that's asked of me. If only we could find something for Papa. But we won't now start trying to sort out everything for ourselves; Eva-Maria is the main thing, and the rest can follow in Act II. I just knew that you'd be trying to move heaven and earth for us, but I hadn't anticipated that something would come up so soon! I only hope that this course proves feasible, and that it gives Eva-Maria the chance to build herself a new life.

It is extremely unlikely that she would be able to find herself a new job here. Do you think that once she's established over there she might then be able to get a permit for an office job that would allow her to use her language, typing and shorthand skills? Could she already put those skills to use at the Cottons'?

Now we just have to hope with all our hearts that our efforts will be paid off. I'm sorry not to be able to enclose a reply coupon for you; this too appears to be fraught with difficulty now, and I won't be able to send them at all in the future. If you don't have the money for postage you'll just have to write fewer letters. We look forward to your next letter with great anticipation, and hope that it won't shatter our dreams.

Loving kisses from Mama

PS By the way, it's possible that we might get the affidavit for America quite soon, but it takes such a long time to get an entry visa that there's absolutely *no way* we could wait here for it to be issued. In England do you think they issue permits for long-term transit? It doesn't seem to be at all clear. Do write and tell me which furniture you were vaguely thinking of for yourself, and which you really don't like. Do you think Mama and Papa might be able to come over very soon after? That would be so wonderful. Of course I haven't mentioned anything to Miss Cotton about them.

[Eva-Maria]

Dear Mouse,

You've really managed to do something rather marvellous there! I take my hat off to you! Now things will change
very quickly for Eva-Maria.

All our very best wishes for the New Year,
and many kisses from your Papa

Georg and Frieda

1939

8 January 1939
Düsseldorf

PARENTS TO EDITH

My dear child,

We're making great progress with our English studies. Erna Böllert and her sister come to us on Tuesday evenings, and we work on our English together. Eva-Maria goes out with the sister quite often. Erna is off to America to get married. She seems much friendlier than she used to be. They no longer live in Brüderstrasse – they were forced to move out!* We've nearly finished the preparations for Eva-Maria's departure, and everything's been organised for you too, hopefully to your satisfaction. – Papa had a dreadful day last Saturday. Since the roots and bone had fused together, they had to drill into his jaw and chisel them out. He has to go back in about ten days. – Who gave you that money? Was it Mrs Mejnen? She wrote to Hilde a short time ago, and said that she would do what she could.

Loving kisses from your Mama

---

* Over the years of the Nazi regime, many Jews were forced to move into smaller and smaller apartments.

Dear Edith,

What a stroke of luck that you're going to get a bit of money again! I so look forward to hearing how your language lessons go. They've now extracted two-thirds of my teeth, so the worst is behind me. That last session was no fun at all. Final act to be played out next week. There's no other news.

Loving kisses,
Papa

13 January 1939
Düsseldorf

GEORG TO EDITH
Dear Edith,

We've just got your letter, which shocked and confused us as I'm sure you can imagine. There are so many different obstacles that prevent emigration at such short notice, but of course there's no reason why you or anyone else over there should be aware of them. There are so many regulations governing the liquidation of assets, and we have to make money available to travel and transport our belongings, and to pay the rather considerable taxes and get permits issued. In Eva-Maria's case, all these matters are relatively straightforward, although much more difficult to arrange than you can possibly imagine. But with Mama and myself, all these obstacles are multiplied to a *very* considerable degree. We'll have to work out how or indeed whether it will be possible to overcome them all, and we are concentrating all our thoughts and activities on this at the moment. We also have to take into account the fact that I have to wait to get a set of dentures fitted. This is unavoidable; without this I wouldn't be able to maintain my good health, and it has to happen in Germany as I'd never be able to raise the costs to have the treatment in England. But this will take several months, and until it is done it will be impossible for me to come over to England. If Mama happens to get herself a position before then, we would have no choice but to let her begin her work, while I'd stay on here and follow later. In that case we'd have to dissolve our household and I'd move into a furnished room. Mama would then be able to start looking around in England for a job for me. Of course I will try to get through the whole process as soon as I can. As the situation stands, you were at any rate quite right to apply for my permit already. I can only be thankful to you for your energy and care. Now we just have to keep on hoping, and try to overcome all these difficulties.

Warmest kisses,
Papa

18 January 1939
Düsseldorf

PARENTS AND EVA-MARIA TO EDITH
Dear Edith,

You are of course quite right when you say that Eva-Maria's prospects are extremely favourable, and if everything works out and she gets her permit we simply cannot be thankful enough. You know that this is what occupies me most at the moment, and I hope with every post that it has been issued. We are still not at all sure what our next step should be, although I absolutely insist that we will not come over to you without knowing how we will be able to live, however modestly. An agency has written to us at Miss d'Avigdor's suggestion, following our letter to her in which we wrote that I intended to take in children who could be tutored by Papa. Remember, we speak 'perfect' English?! – Please answer every single question we ask you! And don't forget to let me know about the electric oven. – I hope you get better really soon, if you're not better already.

A thousand kisses from Mama

My dear old Crocodile,

I'm sorry you're feeling rotten, and I hope you get well soon. My dental treatment cannot be finished any sooner than I've already said; the jaw takes some time to heal after all the teeth have been pulled, and the dentures can't be made and fitted before then.

All the best, and many kisses from Papa

Dear old thing,

We're just listening to Benjamino Gigli on the radio – he's just *fabulous*! Thank heavens that things like that still exist. – I've just had a lesson in English shorthand, and on Wednesday I'm going to start learning English bookkeeping. – I hope your cold isn't too bad and that you're still alive by the time I get to England. You poor worm. But listen, you mustn't worry about Papa; it will all work out eventually. How do you think Mama will cope with those rather foreign English ways?

Get well soon,
your old Eva

As Eva-Maria prepared to emigrate, Georg and Frieda began to consider their own prospects in England with more urgency, particularly after the events of Kristallnacht. *With the help of his daughters, Georg began to write speculative applications to various film companies. The following letters relate to these, and to applications for the various permits required for emigration.*

January 1939
Düsseldorf

FRIEDA AND EVA-MARIA TO EDITH

My dear child,

Eva-Maria is just writing various letters to the contacts you've given us. Do you think there might be a glimmer of hope there somewhere? In any case we'll suggest to those companies that we apply for an information permit so that they'd have the opportunity to meet Papa personally, should they think it necessary. But he can't meet anyone at all for the next few months as he doesn't haven't any teeth. Do we really have to prove to English customs that those things are more than a year old? I haven't kept any of the receipts. You haven't yet written to tell me what *you* might still need. There's a sale starting on 31st, and I could get you some things there.

Do you think you might be able to get the day off on 13 March, and find the money from somewhere to go to Wolfgang's confirmation in Brackley? The poor boy, I can't even send him anything!

A thousand kisses,
Mama

Dear child,

What's the situation with Mama? Has she been put onto Papa's permit application, or how does it work? Many thanks for sending me the list of film companies. There's one thing I don't quite understand. You've written: 'Twickenham Film Studios, 112 St Margaret's Road, Twickenham'. Is that the full address? Do you have to write 'London' as well? Is it a suburb of London? I can't find it on the atlas, and I'm fairly certain the letter won't get there like that.

100000 fat kisses,
your Eva-Maria

1 February 1939
Düsseldorf

FRIEDA TO EDITH

My dear child,

You haven't said anything at all about your cold. Are you back on top form again? I'm delighted that Eva-Maria is making such good progress with all her applications. We think that she'll have all her papers ready here by the end of February at the latest. It always takes a long time, but we've done whatever we can and there's nothing standing in her way at this end – now we just have to hope that everything works out over there! She's always out and about doing things – yesterday she was already at the tax office at seven in the morning, and yet she still had to stand in line until almost eleven o'clock! Dr Bergenthal has got his permit and a house, the lucky man! – I have no doubt it's a good thing that you want to give German lessons, but I'm worried it will all be a bit too much for you. That's something you'll have to work out for yourself, I suppose. Did you ever get Grandma's Christmas parcel? She asked me again because she's not heard a peep from you. – Papa had more teeth pulled last Wednesday – ten at once! It's quite unpleasant, but it went reasonably well and apparently it wasn't too painful. Unfortunately he can now only have liquid, mushy food, which he doesn't really like. But this too will pass.

I had no idea your exams begin already in March. It's so upsetting that the poor boy has to spend the whole of that day with strangers, but if you're busy it obviously can't be helped.

Loving kisses from Mama

2 March 1939
Düsseldorf

GEORG TO EDITH

My dear child,

As usual we were terribly worried to hear news of your cold. We hope that you are being well looked after, and not in too much discomfort. Flu reigns everywhere, and here it has taken an even greater hold than in the Lower Rhine, which is normally known as 'Flu Paradise'. But if you really tackle the illness head-on, you can normally get over it pretty quickly. It's most important that you don't get up too early; that could bring on a relapse which might be even worse than the illness itself. I absolutely insist that you follow my advice as conscientiously as you can. Mama has already written to you about Eva-Maria's permit. We can only hope that it brings her, and indeed all of us, good fortune. So keep your spirits up and get well soon!

                                    Kisses from Papa

                                    22 March 1939
                                    Düsseldorf

PARENTS AND EVA-MARIA TO EDITH
My dear child,

Now you're in the thick of your exams, and I'm thinking of you so much that you *must* be able to sense it. I wish for you that Friday evening will come round again soon, when you can quietly creep into your bed and sleep without a care. Make sure you stay strong and keep yourself together! And if you happen to muck it up, just remember what I've said to you: we'll *still* be able to work something out! Don't forget that, and above all don't drive yourself mad!

Eva-Maria left the house at eight this morning, and we're hoping she'll be issued with her permit today. Then she'll be off to Cologne on Friday to get her visa, and as soon as she gets authorisation to transport her things it's full steam ahead! But now it's *extremely* urgent that we get in touch with those people about the storage – we sent the contract off days ago, and the inspector could arrive any moment. None of us has been able to read the address of the storage place, the way you've written it in your letter, so I'm enclosing it again here. Now you're going to have to do the work yourself and write to them to ask for how long they would be prepared to store things, if the worst came to the worst. If they decide to be difficult about it all, I don't have a clue what we should do. I'd have to cancel all contracts at this end and we wouldn't be able to send everything off when Eva-Maria goes. You won't believe just how complicated everything is, and what a ghastly and tiresome amount of work it all involves. When everything is a bit calmer and you have the time, we'd love to hear about your conversation with Mr Bolton and Wolfgang. I am so happy that Eva-Maria won't be at all far from you. You'll be able to chatter about everything together, and it will make her time at the beginning, the really tough bit, much easier. How lucky we are that you've already been over there for more than two years! Keep your chin up, my dear good child.

Big, big kisses from Mama

My dear Pup,

Break a leg for your exams! When the crisis has abated, please write and tell us in more detail whether you think Wolfgang should stay on at that school.

Loving kisses,
Papa

My dear Edith,

Many thanks for your birthday wishes – I very much hope they will all come true. Now it definitely won't be long before we see each other again. More soon, I've no more time today!

A hundred thousand kisses from your big sister

5 April 1939
Düsseldorf

PARENTS TO EDITH (incomplete)

My dear child,

We still haven't heard anything from you about the shipment. It's high time, now that the inspector has been, and we expect the packing authorisation any day! I would find it dreadfully embarrassing if you can't let us know by return that everything has been arranged. I can't tell you just how difficult it has been to get this far, and I simply couldn't bear the thought that all our work has been in vain! If you still haven't had any response, I beg you to go and complain, and explain to them exactly why we need to know *immediately*. We've decided that Eva-Maria should probably travel sometime around 18 April, and the days are flying by. Yesterday she received a letter from Mrs Perry, which I'm sure she'll tell you about herself. She is quite anxious about going over, and in spite of everything I have to summon all my powers of persuasion to keep her spirits up. All this is just so hard! Hilde got a letter from Mrs Mejnen a few days ago. She's been wondering why she hasn't heard from you for such a long time, and asks whether you've changed your address. I think it's extremely important that you write her a very polite letter – or go and see her if you're in London – and tell her that you haven't been in touch because you've been ill and had exams and lots of work. People want to help you, and it's essential that you keep up good relations with every contact you have. I'm sure there will come a time when Eva-Maria will be pleased to have these people on her side too.

It's Easter already, and this year I can't even send you a little package. Maybe Eva-Maria will be able to bring something over for you later. I hope you have a lovely Easter, and above all that you'll have the chance to rest a bit after the difficult weeks you've just been through.

Loving kisses from Mama

Dear Pup,

Today I've got to bother you with a small task (for a change!), as follows: I wrote to all the film companies on your list, and the only one to reply in a halfway positive manner (even though they were the last to do so) was Twentieth-Century Fox. Their letter was dated 28 February. Even though I wrote in English, they replied in German, signed by a Dr Korth (or Koch, or something like that). He said that they had carefully considered how they might be able to help me out, but it seems that it's almost impossible to provide work opportunities for immigrants . . .

12 April 1939
Düsseldorf

FRIEDA TO EDITH

My dear child,

I was delighted to read your last letter, and I think it has lifted Eva-Maria's spirits again. She's making everything even more difficult for herself – and for us too, if the truth be told – by being fearful of what's about to happen. But I'm certain that your letter has already had a calming influence. I hope you'll both be able to find somebody who would be willing to take on your transport costs; it simply won't be possible to do so from here. What a dreadful pity that you're about to move away from Chislehurst! But it can't be helped, and if you're still able to meet up with each other once in a while – and you at least seem to think that will be possible – then I'm sure you'll both be able to cope. Have you *completely* got over the after-effects of your illness?

Wolfgang got a very good report and Mr Bolton sent a nice letter with it, saying that he was quite happy with him. Now, my dear girl, I hope you have a few peaceful days before the exertion of your move!

Loving kisses from Mama

Eva-Maria joined her sister and brother in England in mid-April 1939, initially staying with the Perry family in London while she looked for work.

30 April 1939
Düsseldorf

GEORG TO EVA-MARIA

My dearest Hen,

We were tremendously happy to get your last two letters – we can tell that your trip went well, and that you're in good spirits. Now to Twentieth-Century Fox business: before you went off on your trip I told you that Edith had made a rather silly omission, in that she hadn't spoken with Dr Korth. I predicted then that Bassler, the boss of the company, would read the manuscript instead of Korth, and would probably send it back. This has now happened. I received the parcel from Bassler yesterday, and he writes: 'This is an interesting tale, but it is only of relevance for Germany. Legal procedure is different here, and the plot therefore loses its point'.

Now I'm afraid you're going to have to speak to Korth and discuss what to do next. In the covering letter I sent off with the manuscript on 19 March, I went into some detail anticipating this particular objection which Bassler has now raised. Do ask Korth to read the letter, as I offer some suggestions as to how you could eliminate these problems. Consider with Korth whether or not I should resubmit the manuscript. If you both decide that I should, I'll send it to you so that you can pass it on. Be brave and be good, and send our good wishes to the Barwicks and the Perrys.

                    Loving kisses from your Papa

3 May 1939
Düsseldorf

PARENTS TO EVA-MARIA

My dearest eldest,

Here's another letter for you, even though I don't know whether or not you're still alive – I haven't had a sign of life from you since Sunday.

The police require a new Certificate of Unobjection-ability from Papa, and as soon as it arrives the shipment can go off. Edith has just written to say she knows of someone who might be able to help us pay for it if it doesn't cost more than seven pounds. It can't possibly, can it? Write and let me know what we should do about mothballing. Grandma has written to Papa's cousins, and I've written to my cousin. When you get to know Mrs Perry a little better, do write and let me know whether I should send something over for her. I hope for post from you tomorrow!

A big fat kiss for today,
Mama

Dear Eva-Maria,

I hope your first few days in your new home have gone well. We think of you often and talk about you a great deal. We so look forward to your next letter.

Warmest kisses,
Papa

5 May 1939
Düsseldorf

PARENTS TO EDITH AND EVA-MARIA

Dearest girls,

I have a feeling you might be reading this letter together, since you wrote saying that Edith would be coming up to town on Saturday. So both of you close your eyes tight, and imagine that I am with you and you can see me. I'll be thinking of you both so much all day that you'll probably get quite a fright. I can just imagine you both chattering away, and I doubt your mouths are still even for a minute. You've got so much to catch up on.

Now to something that's very important to us all: Herr Buse told us that by his reckoning the total weight is probably not more than one and a half to two tonnes. So we're confident that we'll be able to raise the money, thanks to Edith. The person who's offered to pay has set a maximum of seven pounds, and it shouldn't even cost that much. Let's hope that solves that particular problem. As soon as the certificates arrive we'll arrange for the shipment to go off, and we'll let you know when it has.

I hope very much that you have settled in well by now, dear Eva-Maria, and that you've got used to the food. Please make sure that you eat properly; you know how dreadful you look when you let yourself get too thin and pale. If only I knew that you were getting an income from somewhere, at least so that you could write to us regularly. Your letters are my very lifeblood! I've written to my cousin and asked him to send you the reply coupons he wanted to give me. I simply couldn't ask more of him so soon – I don't even know the man! Maybe one day he'll offer something of his own accord. Here the weather is beautiful at the moment, and I hope it's picked up a bit over there too. – Am I right in thinking that you're going to see Wolfgang next week? I'm going to write to him a bit later today. By the way, I recently spoke to Egon Katzenberg on the telephone, and he wants you to send them your address. He's thinking of going over to London soon, and hopes to be able to meet up with you. You should see him if you can. His mother is supposed to be coming out of hospital at the beginning of next week. Isn't that great news! So, my girls, please write and let me know what you get up to.

Hugs and kisses,
Mama

Dear children,

I hope you have a lovely day together. Eva-Maria, please remember all the things I told you regarding Wolfgang and his future schooling; get in touch with Miss d'Avigdor first, and then with Ursula Hirsch (Society of Friends).

Kisses to you both from your Papa

9 May 1939
Düsseldorf

FRIEDA TO EVA-MARIA
My dear child,

I had thought that you might have written us a few lines together on Saturday, and I'm dreadfully disappointed not to have had anything from you yet. Aunt Bertha and Uncle Josi left yesterday lunchtime, so now we have our empire all to ourselves!

Aunt Tilly is really very unwell, so I've offered to help out a bit on a regular basis. Do send her a little letter again soon, if you can. I now won't be able to send off that parcel for Mrs Perry; I'm sure you'll have heard about the new regulations.* What a shame she's so forgetful! She's going to have to do without her scarf for the time being, then. I'd also have liked to send her something edible, but now that's no longer possible.

It's a huge relief for us that you're having such a happy time over there. Of course you have to help Mrs Perry out whenever you can. Unfortunately, if she doesn't make any demands of you, you're likely to feel even more obliged to lend a hand. I'm sure you're well aware that it can only benefit you in the long run if you show your gratitude to people who have taken you on and been kind to you.

We got a letter from Wolfgang today. It's wonderful that you'll be able to go and see him on Sunday. Don't you think it would be proper if you wrote to Mr Bolton in advance to say that you're coming, and that Wolfgang is going to be spending the day with you? It's just a formality, but better for Wolfgang if you do it that way! – How did Edith look when you saw her?

It's now Wednesday, and I haven't heard a peep from the

---

* From May 1939, presents sent abroad by Jews had to be approved by the customs authorities.

two of you. The Hamachers came over yesterday, so I couldn't finish this letter. And now I'm a little concerned as the post has been and I still haven't heard from you. I spend my time waiting from one post to the next; it's enough to drive me up the wall. I just got a letter from Aunt Bertha saying they got home safely. She also wrote that Martha Casalta sadly died on Monday, which was in fact her birthday. She's almost the last of the older generation, and her death brought back many old memories from my childhood.

I'm knitting jumpers for the Hamacher boys – they all seem to have their birthdays around this time. I've finished Uncle Josi's, and it's turned out really well. If Mrs Perry likes your clothes so much, I could always knit her something too. I think your shipment will be going off at the beginning of next week; all the documents are ready apart from the import licence. Anyway, that's all for today – I'm holding my breath for the post, and hope that nothing's gone astray.

A big fat kiss from your Mama

My dear Hen,

I enclose two copies of Wolfgang's school report, one for Miss d'Avigdor and the other for Ursula Hirsch, if you think it appropriate. I hope we'll get post from you tomorrow.

Kisses from Papa

12 May 1939
Düsseldorf

FRIEDA TO EVA-MARIA

My dearest eldest,

Letters have just arrived from both of you at last – I've been longing for them so. It's wonderful that you spent such a lovely day together, and that you could finally have a really good chat about everything. I'm delighted you'll be able to go and see Wolfgang again, and it's probably a good idea to talk to him after you've had your conversation with Miss d'Avigdor. Do you know something? I think it would be lovely if you could find some work which would enable you and Wolfgang to live together in a nice quiet little room somewhere until he finishes his schooling. Then he would always have a home to go to. You'd be able to talk things through properly, and after all you've got everything over there that you'd need to set up a small household. I'd be so much happier if I knew you were both together. It's a terrible shame that it seems so completely impossible for you to get a job in an office, but it can't be helped. And you have to understand that it was still necessary for you to go over. I'm convinced you'll find some kind of employment soon, whereas here there would have been nothing for you at all. I'm sure you know all this, but sometimes you have to remind yourself that this is the way it had to be, and from now on you should only really tackle life from the angle that's presented to you. I'm sure it must be awkward for you that the Perrys are so extraordinarily pious, but think about it this way: it's better to have too much devotion than too little! It's because of this that they feel so responsible towards their fellow human beings; I'm sure they'll be there to help you out wherever they can. I do think it's very kind of Mr Perry to give you two shillings. In our present circumstances we have to be grateful for every little bit of support that's offered to us. If people don't have the means, then of course they can't help. As far as Ursula Hirsch is concerned, you should do exactly as you've suggested. If you do get the chance to speak to her, you should be quite open about everything – that's always the best way.

We were always aware that the Hodgkins' guarantee was a mere formality.* In fact they wrote to us a few weeks ago. Luckily you weren't at home at the time, so we were able to keep the letter secret until you left for England. I thought that if you read it, you'd find it even more difficult to leave home.

You know I'd be happy to take on any kind of work. Have you asked yet whether I might be able to get some training at a hospital, or am I already too old?

It's dreadfully cold here. The heating has gone out and I'm freezing to death. – You mustn't worry about us. We'll wait patiently for our time to come, and until then we're with you in all our thoughts.

.A thousand warm kisses from Mama

---

* This may refer to the affidavit that a German emigrant would need to secure from a contact in England, giving assurance that accommodation would be provided on entry, if necessary.

12 May 1939
Düsseldorf

GEORG TO EVA-MARIA
Dear Eva-Maria,

The Hodgkin–Mejnen affair has one advantage, and that is to show you how often sheer fraud (there's no other way to describe it) is perpetrated in matters concerning emigration, even by people you'd never expect it of. You can see that in these situations you have to be more prudent than usual.

There's no point in sending you the rejection letters, but if you want to go and have a meeting with the one company that's shown an interest, then please only do so after you've spoken to Dr Korth. He might be able to give you some advice, whereas if you went and saw anyone else now, it might be a complete waste of time.

Kisses from Papa

12 May 1939
Düsseldorf

FRIEDA TO EDITH
My dearest Edith,

Every day I've been waiting for a few lines about your time together, and until now I've been disappointed. But your long letter has arrived at last, and I'm happy again. It's wonderful that you had so much fun on the Saturday. How on earth did they both manage to get there so dreadfully late? You were brilliant to make them believe they were meeting up with you alone. I can imagine that you laughed your heads off, and it probably did you all lots of good – laughing is so healthy. It made me terribly happy to read all about your lovely late-birthday, post-exam celebration. It would be wonderful if Eva-Maria could come and stay with you for a few days over Whitsun. It can't be easy for her to be living in that rather peculiar atmosphere.

I immediately wrote to Uncle Paul about your holidays and asked him if you could come and stay. As you know it's his birthday tomorrow, 13 May, so I leapt at the opportunity. Unfortunately it will be impossible for you to do the same this year as last, so I'd be very relieved if you could go and see them instead of having to take on temporary work. I think you could really do with a period of complete relaxation.

Do you not know of anyone who might be able to arrange for me to do some training in midwifery at a hospital? Or maybe even as a lying-in or infant nurse? That's the area I'd prefer to work in, but of course I'll do anything!

> So, my girl, farewell for now,
> and a big kiss from your Mama

> *16 May 1939*
> *Berlin*

AUNT BERTHA TO EVA-MARIA

Dearest Eva-Maria,

Let's talk about you, my little love. It's hard for a child when there's no one there to hold her in their arms or sit her on their lap, and no one's helping my little girl, poor thing.

But I certainly won't give up all hope, and I'll always believe that in the end that kindly hand you've so longed for will appear and grant all your wishes, both big and small. I'm glad that you feel quite comfortable at the Perrys otherwise. I think everyone over there is rather devout. Only yesterday at my dear Aunt Olga's birthday party I was talking to a young girl who's going to England next week, and she told me all her friends had written to her saying that they have to go to church at least twice a day! Well, at least you don't have to do it for ever. In any case you should be glad that you're away from here and in reachable distance of your siblings. Your mother wrote me a long letter yesterday telling me all about the time you spent with Edith. I can just imagine you both nattering away, and I bet your mouths weren't still for a minute.

Just after you left here I did my very best to cheer your mother up, and thank God I was more or less successful. Bit by bit she became quite cheerful again, and by the time we left she'd also been reassured by your sweet letter. I tried to make it clear to her that she'll still have to look after Papa just as she did before, and even sit with him while he's working and go for walks with him regularly. She'll have to entirely transfer her energies and attentions to him. Our best plan of all, if it's workable, would be to try to find a suitable apartment in Berlin for them to move into. First thing tomorrow I've got to go to the council offices anyway on my sister's behalf, and I can ask them whether a move into the area from another city is even allowed. Papa thoroughly approves of our plan, but he says he'd prefer to move to a suburb so that he could go for a good walk every day. It would of course be the best solution, and it would make your Mama's separation from the three of you that much easier to bear, especially now that it seems highly unlikely that they'll be able to follow you over there.

Yesterday we got a long letter from Peter. He writes that warm winds are now blowing, and that they're spending the nights out in the woods; apparently the heat is unbearable inside the house. Sadly he didn't manage to get to that wedding in Tel Aviv; the authorities refused him a visa. Uncle Leo went to all kinds of trouble imaginable, but because of the unrest there's a ban on all travel organised through the Jugend Alijah.* Even though I hate to say it, I'm rather glad it turned out that way – I wouldn't like to think of Peter being in any danger. But he was extremely disappointed by it all, and I wouldn't have wanted to begrudge him that pleasure. Hopefully peace will soon settle in over there, and he'll be able to take some time off.

By the way, Uncle Richard heard yesterday that the hearing went rather badly over there. His cousin has been forced to sell his house, and he's in the worst possible situation financially. He wrote to say that if Uncle Richard still wants to come, he's going to have to see about getting himself some work because he can't support him. Aunt Mathilde is going to stay in Belgium, whatever happens, at least until Uncle Richard is in a position to provide for her.

---

* The Jugend Alijah movement was founded in 1933 by Recha Freier to support the emigration of Jewish children and young people to Palestine. The methods she used to get children out of Germany were regarded by some as illegal.

It's of course desperately sad for both of them, but what else can they do?

How is Edith getting on? Does she like it in the new home? Have you already been to see Wolfgang? I'll try to get hold of a reply coupon for you. If I don't succeed, please don't bother writing to us directly any more, but send a note via your parents instead. So, my little one, be brave and be good. You're the eldest after all, and you have to set the best possible example for the others. Give my love to Edith and Wolfgang.

Warmest greetings and kisses,

Aunt Bertha

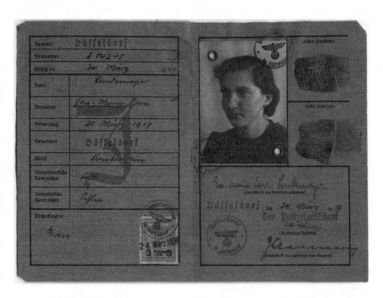

Eva-Maria's ID card issued in 1939. As with all Jewish females, the name Sara was added to her existing names. Also note the letter 'J' denoting the Jewish identity of the holder.

17 May 1939
Düsseldorf

FRIEDA TO EVA-MARIA

My dearest eldest,

I've just found some English translations of your references and Papa has packed them up for the post. Do you think you might be able to use them?! It was lovely to get long letters from you both yesterday and today. It always puts me into a good mood for the rest of the day. But each time I get a letter I always think about all the money you've spent on postage. You should have bought yourself something to eat instead!

I'm sure you can understand why we didn't want to tell you about the whole Hodgkin thing before you left. But there's one other issue which I won't keep from you any longer, even though we knew about this too at the time. The affidavit is only valid until November 1939. As it's a complete impossibility that we'll be over there by then, it's going to be rather ineffective for us too; apparently you can only get it extended if you have a date for a hearing. We'll have to write to them and see what happens.

It was most sensible of you to go off to the park that time. You do need to have a bit of sun, and I hope the weather finally improves so that you can do it more often. What a shame I can't hear the singing Perry family plus their parrot, even just once! Should Papa or I write a few lines to Mr or Mrs Perry sometime? Grete's birthday is on 3 July, but I don't know Hilde Wegner's.

What a *great* pity that Miss d'Avigdor is no longer at Inter-Aid! I think it's out of the question that Wolfgang would be able to pass his exams at Christmas. It would be wonderful, certainly, but quite impossible. If only we could find some-body to pay his school fees. He can even become a farmer later, if that's what he wants, but first he really must learn something substantial. When are you going to Brackley? It's wonderful that you had such a nice time there recently, despite the rain, and especially pleasing that W. is looking so well. You don't think he's getting too fat, do you?

I'm glad the woollen underwear has been so useful, but I hope you won't be needing it for much longer. Papa's new teeth have been delayed by another three weeks. – I was thrilled to read that that English fellow was so impressed with your English. I don't want you to even contemplate the whole Brussels thing. For all kinds of reasons you should stay in England, and I certainly don't want you going to Belgium. It's so sweet that you'd be prepared to take on that job, even though I'm sure you wouldn't enjoy it at all. Papa thinks that there are no real opportunities over there, and that you should be content to stay where you are. One day you'll get a job just like that! You really have to take your time and not rush things. You know that we can be patient people, and we'd much prefer to wait until you find something that won't be too strenuous for you, if I can put it like that.

Here's a big fat kiss from your Mama

21 May 1939
Düsseldorf

GEORG TO EVA-MARIA [incomplete]
Dear child,
I enclose a copy of my curriculum vitae, which I've sent

off to Demuth together with the covering letter he asked for.
Glücksmann is going to send him a letter of recommendation, and on his advice I've also sent Demuth the printed
version of my treatise. I told him that you'd be forwarding
an English translation of the curriculum vitae . . .

*The following letter appears in English in the German
edition of this book, translated on Georg Lindemeyer's
behalf, and has been left in its original form.*

Dear Sirs,

I herewith beg to apply for employment in your firm. I
intend to emigrate to England and should like very much to
work in the film-industry. I think, I am fitted for this branch
in a special measure, as I have been engaged many years
with the international film- and copyright and also with
literature, especially with dramaturgy.

In 1931 I published a big treatise about the international
film-, patent- and copyright: 'Expropriation and legal licence in the sphere of the copyright' ('Enteignung und
gesetzliche Lizenz auf dem Gebiet des Urheberrechts') in
the archives for copy-, film- and theatre-right 1931. I just
have published (in November 1938) another big treatise
'Publishing rights as guarantee' ('Sicherheitsleistung durch
Bestellung von Verlagsrechten') in the international juridical periodical 'Copyright' appearing in Leiden (Holland). It
is written in the German language with an English and
French summary. I can send you a copy if you wish.

Meanwhile other treatises have been published in other juridical periodicals. Now I am working at an even bigger treatise 'To the theory of the law of licence' ('Zur Theorie der Lizenzrechte'), that concerns the sphere of the patent- and copyright.

In 1931 I wrote a film-comedy. The manuscript has a great approbation in its special circles. The firm of production, that took a great interest in my comedy, could not execute it, for the only reason, that it got into financial difficulties.

I have been engaged for a number of years with a work 'Critical dramaturgy' ('Kritische Dramaturgie'). The first volume is finished and the second has reached an advanced stage. In this work the dramas of poets of all countries and times are analysed. Experts to whom I read the manuscript, all expressed their great approbation.

The long and very detailed occupation with the drama-turgy enables me to criticize and remodel film manuscripts. I am especially able to propose the fitting stuffs for filming and if necessary to remodel them for this purpose, as I have a most voluminous knowledge in European literature and European history. Since my childhood till now I have, without interruption, made an exhaustive study of European history.

I know English and French. During the Great War I was an interpreter in the French language. I also know Latin and Greek. Now I am learning book-keeping.

I am fifty-one years old; since my fifth year of life I am a member of the protestant religion. My wife is protestant too and my children were born and grown up protestant. From

1915 to 1933 I was a lawyer in Düsseldorf (Germany). In 1933 I had to give up practising because of the race-laws. Besides the jurisprudence I also have studied history, philosophy and history of art.

I have three children. The two youngest are in school in England, having been there two years. My eldest daughter will probably emigrate to England in a short time as companion to a Rector's wife in Yorkshire and also to teach German, French and Spanish languages.*

I can give you some personal references. I am able to give you the address of our clergyman and other people, if you wish. Would you please answer me, if my presentation in your firm would be essential, that I can try to get a visa.

I should be very grateful, if a position in any capacity could be found for me in your firm, and you may be sure that I shall do my best to prove a useful and capable member of your staff.

Meanwhile I await your favourable reply and am dear Sirs

Yours faithfully
Georg Lindemeyer

When the Inter-Aid Committee were no longer able to finance Wolfgang's education, Mr Bolton, the headmaster at Magdalen College School, refused to keep him on there after the summer of 1939. With the intervention of Inter-Aid

* This letter was clearly written before Eva-Maria's move to England. The position in Yorkshire referred to here was probably with the Cotton family, who offered the original guarantee to assist Eva-Maria's emigration.

and his parents, however, Mr Bolton changed his mind to allow Wolfgang to stay on until Christmas, but in the interim this became a matter of great concern to Frieda and Georg Lindemeyer, as the following letters show.

23 May 1939
Düsseldorf

GEORG TO EVA-MARIA

Dear Eva-Maria,

I find Mr Bolton's rejection of Wolfgang very painful indeed, even though I suppose we should have expected it. I thought that he might at least have shown a little more willing. If he had, I would have written to various people in England asking for financial help for Wolfgang's schooling from Christmas onwards. Now that Bolton has adopted this completely negative attitude, I have to admit that Mama is right; it would be a mistake to keep Wolfgang at the school without Bolton's full support. He will try to prove to us that he assessed the boy correctly, and this will achieve nothing useful – in fact it could be damaging. But now we can't consider sending Wolfgang to another school. The Inter-Aid Committee wouldn't go along with this, and for Wolfgang it would mean going through another difficult readjustment. So our only option would be to send him to a technical college. First of all we need to know how much that might cost, secondly how we would find the money, and, thirdly, where would Wolfgang live? Those are my current thoughts on the matter. Perhaps I'll have a clearer picture of the situation tomorrow or the day after, and I'll

write to you again. In the meantime I'd be grateful if you
could do anything you think might be helpful in all this.

Kisses from Papa

23 May 1939
Düsseldorf

FRIEDA TO EVA-MARIA

My dear child,

I only meant to write again after four weeks! – It's
regrettable that you weren't able to get anywhere at all
with Mr Bolton, but it was to be predicted, and do you
know something? I'm not even sure that he's completely
wrong. Wolfgang is definitely more suited to practical work
than to studying, so our hope for his future successes should
be enhanced by the fact that he's managed to get such
decent results through sheer hard work and application. Of
course we can't stop thinking about what might be best for
the life of the child, and it's quite possible that if we keep
concentrating on this we might come up with another
solution.

At the moment I also believe that it would be equally
wrong to put pressure on Miss Barshall at Inter-Aid to try
and get something out of her. It is probably much more
important that we set all the wheels in motion in good time
so that Wolfgang can get an apprenticeship as close to you
as possible, and one which would also enable him to attend
evening classes. He's a healthy, strong lad, and there's no
reason why he shouldn't be able to do all those things that
other boys can. I'm so delighted that you are able to stand in

for me as far as your little brother is concerned, and that you're over there now so you can talk to him about all the important issues that concern his career. I wouldn't try to force a longer stay at the school, not through Ursula Hirsch, Pastor Frank or anyone else. Then the poor boy *definitely* wouldn't have a good time there! Hilde also has asked me to send you her regards. She's 'madly' busy, and at the moment she's upstairs doing some shorthand. I think she's finding it rather difficult. She said she'd write to you as soon as she has a moment. Ruth turned up here at three o'clock on Sunday. The two of us had a coffee here first, and then we went for a walk. She took my arm – just like Eva-Maria, she said. I have to say, I was rather touched by all her sacrifice. That's all for now!

A thousand kisses,
Mama

25 May 1939
Düsseldorf

PARENTS TO EVA-MARIA

My dear girl,

The prospects do indeed seem to be quite hopeful, but I won't quite believe it yet – I'd find the disappointment too hard to bear. So let's wait patiently until the end of the week, and then we'll know whether or not Rev. Edwards sent a letter at all! If it's something that Papa has to go over to England to look into, you will of course have to tell him what a trip like that would entail. Our radio is being repaired at the moment. There was too much interference so we decided to take it in. The antenna is rather loose, and so is one of the knobs, and there are various other things wrong with it. – I'll be very happy to get it back again. Otherwise there's no news really. Frau Hamacher now goes with little Ingrid (who you met at that Swiss lady's house) and another friend to the cinema every Wednesday, and then they go out afterwards for a coffee. They're not home before midnight, by which time her sensible husband has already had half a night's sleep. But I suppose it makes a bit of a change. What are you going to be doing over the holiday? Will you be able to see Edith? We're going to stay quietly at home, and in our thoughts we'll always be together with you.

A big fat Whitsun kiss from your Mama

Dear Eva-Maria,

Your news about Reverend Edwards is most interesting. We'll just have to wait and see how things develop. I'm still thinking a great deal about Wolfgang's future. I would very much like him to attend a technical college. Mama is of a different opinion, and thinks that he would be better off starting an apprenticeship straight away; he'd then be able to learn by experience and pick up his theoretical education by going to evening classes. I'm sure that's right, and I'm well aware that my own experience was defined by the German way of teaching, which always puts more emphasis on theoretical training than on practice. In England, quite rightly, they attach greater value in educational terms to practical experience.

I also concede that a young man like Wolfgang might get a great deal more out of practical work, whereas purely theoretical study might well tire him more easily, and perhaps even disillusion him. On the other hand I think it's also crucial that a technical college could provide him with a certificate equivalent to that awarded by Magdalen College. Then he'll have got himself a qualification which would stand him in good stead for the rest of his life. Mama doesn't quite agree with me, but in my opinion that's why we have to find out whether Wolfgang could attend that kind of college, and above all whether we'll be able to raise the money to pay for it. I don't think that's going to be at all easy, but we have to at least make the effort, however difficult and embarrassing this might be. What do you think about all this, and what does everyone else over there think? This is certainly no easy task that we've now burdened you with, especially as you have your own future and ours to worry about too. But at the moment we have no choice, and even though this is a huge responsibility which will require a great deal of effort on your part, perhaps you'll also find some satisfaction in the knowledge that you're contributing in such a crucial way to this important issue. When parents are no longer alive, it is often an older sister who has to take the place of both the mother and father for her younger siblings. Luckily it's not quite as grim as all that, but you're going to have to summon up a similar kind of energy as that required in such a situation. I wish you a happy Whitsun, and hope you have a nice holiday.

Kisses from your Papa

30 May 1939
Düsseldorf

PARENTS TO EVA-MARIA

My dearest eldest,

So the holidays are over! I was supposed to spend the whole of the first day with the Böllerts and go on a boat trip to Emmerich, but the weather was simply impossible. Papa was invited for lunch with Frau Hohaus, so I could easily have gone, but I wouldn't have enjoyed the trip at all with all the wind and the cold. Yesterday we set off for Kaiserswerth at eleven, and walked from there to Wittlaer. You should by now have got the card we sent from there. We were back here by three, and that was probably a good thing as there were so many people out in the fine weather. I think it's very sweet of the Perrys to offer to put Papa up too – they do seem to be particularly lovely people. But sadly it probably won't be necessary for Papa to come over to England on a research trip; we haven't yet heard a word from Rev. Edwards. We simply cannot give up hope, even if everything seems really very difficult and we sometimes feel we can't go on.

All you can ask of Inter-Aid is that they try to find a decent apprenticeship for Wolfgang in London itself, so that he's near to you, and then you can ask them about evening classes too. See whether they can sort all that out, or whether you'll have to do it. – It's an awful shame that you can't get together with Edith just because of this stupid money situation – I'm afraid I really can't help from here, and I don't know what to suggest. Lony is coming to see us later. In two weeks' time Ilse P. is going off on holiday to the same place she was at last summer. She said she'd write to you sometime soon.

A thousand kisses,
Mama

My dear old Hen,

If our plan with Rev. Edwards and Religious Film Ltd doesn't work out, it's probably because they're looking for someone who will be able to help with actual film production. Of course you'd need practical experience of the film industry for that, which I don't have. But I can read through film scripts and edit them, and I can even sort out copyright issues. There must be those kinds of jobs around too.

As far as Wolfgang is concerned, I had thought to ask Freer and Finnit whether they might be able to raise the funds in their particular parishes to send him to a technical school. However, Mama has kept me from doing so, quite rightly – she says you can't put the goodwill of these clergymen to such a test, and that if they'd wanted to help out they would already have taken steps to do so. If your discussions with Ellen or anybody else throw up the possibility that W. might still be able to go to a normal school, of course there's no reason why that shouldn't happen, even if the people at Inter-Aid have already begun to look for an apprenticeship place. Fräulein Böllert has just arrived and now she's helping Mama with the drying-up.

Warm kisses,
Papa

31 May 1939
Düsseldorf

PARENTS TO EVA-MARIA

Dear Eva-Maria,

I'm quickly writing this card to you so that you get an answer to your letter by return. Of course we can't say what your chances are of getting a decent job in London. I can well believe there's a great deal to be said for accepting the Plymouth job, but it's just impossible for us to weigh up the pros and cons from here. Considering all the objections you've raised, I do think it would be much better for you to stay in London, but it depends above all on how long the Perrys are still prepared to put you up, and whether you can afford to wait until you find the right job there. That is of course the cardinal issue. It's lovely that you're going to see Edith. If you've got the money, just do it.

A thousand kisses,
Mama

Dear Eva-Maria,

If the Perrys are happy to keep you on and you think you might still be able to get a job in London, then turn down Plymouth. You should go and see Edith in any case.

Warmest wishes,
Papa

FRIEDA TO EDITH AND EVA-MARIA
My dear girls,

I only wish we'd been born into the world a little later, when television would reach a stage when we could see across huge distances and I'd be able to watch you both laughing and sounding off about things, but also discussing all the serious issues on which so very much depends. I do find it hugely disappointing that Religious Film hasn't been in touch at all. After we got Edith's hopeful letter I had a vision of the five of us sitting happily around a coffee table in London. Perhaps something else will crop up soon, but in the meantime, dear Eva-Maria, you've scored such a great success that we should really be quite satisfied and happy. The fact that Wolfgang will now be able to stay on at the school until Christmas is such a tremendous stroke of luck that we just can't be thankful enough. We'll send a little note to Miss Barshall later today. Should we write to Bolton too? I'm not so sure! What do you think? Now of course he's going to have to pull himself together and show he's really making an effort, and getting somewhere too. Obviously if Papa had contacts in film companies things would be very different. But where on earth are we going to find them at this stage? Papa will write himself about everything else. He went to the dentist again today, only to be told that they still can't start treatment because some areas haven't healed properly yet. What shall we do about the affidavit? The period of validity is written on the left at the bottom of the page. Should I still get a photocopy made, or isn't there any point? Do I need to get copies made of both registration numbers, or will one be enough? I'll get it done as soon as I hear back from you. Ruth surprised me at about seven o'clock on Wednesday, and she joined us on our Wednesday outing. Hilde is coming to see us this evening, and tomorrow afternoon at 3.20 I'm meeting up with Lony Böllert. We think we might go for a walk, and then pay a visit to Fräulein Peters sometime in the afternoon. You can see that I'm not wasting away. Now try to imagine that I have one arm around each of you, and that I'm hugging and kissing you to death,

                                                        Mama

                                                        6 June 1939
                                                        Düsseldorf

FRIEDA TO EVA-MARIA

My dear girl,

Your last letter has just arrived. Yes, I can imagine that was a huge disappointment, only being able to see each other for such a short time. But it may be that this noble stoicism will produce some kind of fruit, and you might have achieved something already in today's discussion! I'm glad of course that the whole business with Religious Film isn't completely over and done with. We have to grab at these little threads of hope – we can't give up entirely. There has to be at least one solution.

But now to Wolfgang! You of all people will know how delighted we were to hear that he could stay on until Christmas, but now he's just written to say that Bolton has been causing problems again and – just as I predicted – has been foiled by Inter-Aid. Papa wrote to Miss Barshall a few days ago to thank her. Could you translate the enclosed letter to Bolton into decent English and send it off to him as soon as possible? Papa is just writing the German version, and he won't be adding to this letter so that we can get it off to you by airmail straight away. Don't you think it would be a good idea if you went back to Miss Barshall and asked her to keep Wolfgang there until Christmas, whatever Bolton thinks? At this stage there's so little time that he might only be able to get himself a second-rate apprentice-ship.

By Christmas you and Edith will surely be earning a bit of money, and Papa too perhaps. You should both be able to contribute enough for him to be able to stay there until the end of his schooling after all. You should just speak to Miss Barshall as openly as you can. It's just awful, I can't stop worrying about all this, and we're just going to have to wait and see what happens with the rest of it. Worst of all is that I have to sit here uselessly, unable to do anything to help!

On Saturday I went to the Pappelwald with Lony, and then dropped in on Ilse P. She's gone off now. When Edith stays with Uncle Paul, she'll probably hear from her there. She's got an absolutely beautiful blue headscarf, and she's generally rather well equipped for bad weather. Now I'm desperate to read your next letter, and so hope that you spent a lovely day together.

A thousand fat kisses from your Mama

6 June 1939
Düsseldorf

GEORG TO MR BOLTON

Dear Mr Bolton,

Today, in a letter from Wolfgang, we heard that the Inter-Aid Committee has asked you to keep him at the school until Christmas, and to give him his certificate then. He went on to say that you will be unable to give him his certificate at Christmas, and that you have asked Inter-Aid to remove him from the school now. Of course we understand that it is unreasonable to expect that Wolfgang should receive his certificate so soon, but despite this I beg you with all my heart to keep the boy on at the school at least until then. He has now proven to you that he has a strong desire to learn. What is more, our daughters will almost certainly have paid jobs by Christmas. Edith, a trainee in Horam, has passed her Class II exams, and her contract there expires on 15 December this year, leaving her free to take on a paid job. I am certain that Eva-Maria will find a job even sooner. Both sisters will then be able to contribute to the costs of Wolfgang's schooling, and we may also have found somebody who will take on the remainder of the fees.

Dear Mr Bolton, we well understand that in arriving at your decision you have only thought of what's best for the boy. But we beg you with all our hearts to make a concession on this issue; Wolfgang's entire future depends on it. You have said in the past that we can count on your sympathy in our difficult situation. Please allow this sympathy to prove itself through action, and come to the help of these parents who have now been separated from their son for so long, and can do nothing more for him but worry and beg favours on his behalf.

With many kind regards to you and Mrs Bolton from my wife and myself.

Yours very sincerely
Georg Lindemeyer

10 June 1939
Düsseldorf

GEORG TO EVA-MARIA
Dear Hen,

I enclose the letter from Bolton, and a carbon of my letter to Korth. Please send Bolton's letter back to us when you next write. Could you go to the Inter-Aid Committee and do everything you can to get them to agree to Bolton's plan of keeping W. on at the school until July 1940, when he'll be awarded his certificate. It may be that we'll be able to find someone to contribute to the fees from Christmas this year onwards. The timing is now crucial, so get going! Following your suggestions I have written to Edwards, and I've also sent a thank-you note to Bolton. Mama and Ruth are just brewing up the translation next door in the dining room, much helped by the prevailing heat. We'll still get the letter off today.

Now to the main point of my letter, which I'm discreetly adding at the end: your things will be packed up and loaded next Friday (16 vi). The Deutsche Bank managed to delay this by five weeks, by submitting incorrect applications and making all kinds of other errors. What is more, we now have the pleasure of being allowed to pay another 60 Marks, which is how much the conveyance costs have risen by since 1 May. We'll let you know when the shipment is due to arrive in London.

Warmest kisses,

Papa

10 June 1939
Düsseldorf

FRIEDA TO EVA-MARIA
My dear child,

It's sad that you had to cut short your stay with Edith, and you still didn't get the job. Well, if Edwards went through with his plan of taking you on to do housework and some administration, things would be different. But since the house hasn't even been bought yet, it will probably be a long time before you'll be able to start work. Can't he employ you now as his wife's domestic, but for the time being get you to work more in his office while there's still not enough for you to do in the house? The Cottons' idea has probably got a great deal going for it because they're such nice people, but you'll have to consider it very carefully as you'd be such a long way from London. If you went and stayed up there for a month on holiday, I'm sure it would do your health a great deal of good. Edwards hasn't written to us, but according to your wishes we have just penned the most brilliant letter, and when he gets it he'll probably want to employ our entire family! – I just hope Bolton will be able to get somewhere with Inter-Aid. He's certainly right in saying that a quarter of a year would just be a waste of time for Wolfgang, and that the whole thing only makes sense if he stays until July 1940. Let's keep our fingers crossed!

Edith wrote saying she got sunstroke in Eastbourne – apparently she got a dreadful headache and even vomited. How could she have been stupid enough to lie in the sun when she knows she can't take it? – You left here six weeks ago yesterday! Let's hope that this long wait produces some results soon. If I knew that we were getting somewhere, I'd be quite happy to go on waiting, even if it's not exactly pleasant.

Warmest kisses from Mama

17 June 1939
Düsseldorf

FRIEDA TO EVA-MARIA

My dear child,

Your letter came today, after I'd spent a whole week worrying dreadfully about you both. Now I'm comforted again, especially as Edith seems to be better. On top of everything else I heard that Wolfgang had an attack of scarlet fever while he was playing cricket. He had to spend eight days in an isolation ward with several others, and it seems he's now fully recovered so I can breathe easily again. I'll send the photographs back to you tomorrow. I thought they were delightful, and now I hope for speedy replacements. It definitely appears as though you've got a bit chubbier, or is that just the way it looks? I entirely agree with everything Papa has said about the 'Wolfgang issue'. On no account should we attempt to get Wolfgang to sit the exams at Christmas. On the contrary, it would be extremely welcome news if they decided they could keep him on for the two extra terms from Christmas until July. He's certainly been making a huge effort. Perhaps you could also mention to Miss Barshall that he got a prize for French last year, and in both Latin and Mathematics. And just think, he couldn't speak a single word of English when he first arrived there two and a quarter years ago.

Fräulein Peters is still here. The lady she's to work for has been very ill, but she still hopes to be gone from here by 15 July. Have you not yet heard of any possibilities for Lony? Today they're going on a company outing for which they all had to bring along six Marks. She wasn't terribly pleased about that.

What will happen to you when the Perrys go off on their trip?! I think it's so wonderful that they all wanted to take you along. Everything would be much easier if you had another job by then. Yesterday was absolutely exhausting, but I'm relieved that everything went off. They arrived here at 5.30 p.m., but they couldn't start packing anything until an hour later because the customs officials came so late. They were still at it after ten o'clock. I rather wished that you'd still been here, but actually it went fine in the end! I think they packed everything well, with mothballs and all, but of course it shouldn't sit around for too long without being unpacked as the moth powder wears off after a while. I went to see Frau Pastor Homann the other day. They send their very best regards, as do Frau Hohaus and an awful lot of other people.

Now, my treasure, farewell!

A big hug from your Mama

21 June 1939
Düsseldorf

FRIEDA TO EDITH

My dear child,

It's wonderful news that you're feeling better again, but I do have to admonish you this time. I specifically asked you to write me a short note just to tell me that you're better or how you are. I'm sure that with even the tiniest bit of goodwill you would have found the time. Instead I had to spend the entire week worrying dreadfully about you. Unfortunately I didn't get anything from Eva-Maria during that time either, even though normally she writes frequently, so all I could think was that you were terribly ill and that she had come to your bedside. You could have spared me all this worry if you'd only thought to pick up a card and just write: 'I am better'. But now I've gone on at you enough, and I hope with all my heart that you'll never be ill again, and that I'll never have cause to worry about you so much.

I hope that Miss Giles is able to arrange for you to have your holidays a little later, so you can spend as much time as possible with Uncle Paul. It's not really much time for you to relax completely, and every day of it you have to spend in London would be a shame. If you've finished all your training by Christmas and start a proper job, I'm sure you'll find it rather demanding, and you'd have to be healthy and fit in order to manage it all. Do you still intend to work for a time at a hospital, to get that bit of extra training? From this distance I can't really judge what would be best for you, but I imagine it might be quite a good idea, and certainly advantageous to any work you might have in the future.

It's still unclear how things will work out for Wolfgang. Eva-Maria is doing her utmost, but at the moment it seems unlikely that she'll get anywhere. Still, I have great faith in him, and I'm sure he will get to where he wants to be even if we don't succeed in persuading them to keep him at the school. He really has managed to prove to the school that he's hard-working and energetic, and I'm certain it hasn't been at all easy for him to get such respectable results. You probably already know that he got two prizes on Speech Day (Latin and Mathematics). The shipment should be arriving in London tomorrow, and with any luck you should find everything in good condition. I'm sure Eva-Maria has told you that it didn't weigh very much in the end, so the transport costs you need to get together will be much lower than we'd all thought. It would be wonderful if Eva-Maria could get herself a room somewhere soon so that she'd be able to store everything and begin to use it. Then we wouldn't have to take advantage of the generosity of the storage people, and also things don't get damaged half as much through use as they do in storage. Most important of all you'd then have a proper home to go to when you have time off. You say that we write so little about ourselves in our letters: well, my child, we are only thinking of you, and so little has happened in my own life since you've all been gone that it simply wouldn't be worth writing about. I go out only rarely. What I like to do most is sit in my little corner and sew or knit, or occupy myself some other way, or listen to the radio. I'm always rather glad when nothing really happens, because news is generally not good news. My only bit of diversion comes with the postman, and my only joy is when he brings a letter from one of you.

A big fat kiss from Mama

22 June 1939
Düsseldorf

FRIEDA TO EVA-MARIA
My dear girl,

The letter with Wolfgang's reports has gone off to Miss Barshall with the same post, registered. I have to say that I'm not exactly delighted at this course of events, but we haven't actually expressed this in the letter, and now we've just got to take the chance. Hopefully he'll be on his best behaviour in London and at least give them a favourable impression, so they might decide to help him out even if he doesn't manage to pass his exams. I think it's complete madness that we should have to torment the poor boy like this, and it's such a tragedy to be so entirely excluded from the education of your own child. It goes totally against my nature to have to stand idly by when I can so clearly see that the life of my child could be directed along other paths which would prove to be better for his future. But I'm just going to have to come to terms with this, as with everything else.

Can you believe that Papa has agreed to read *Effi Briest* with me some day?* It's quite wonderful. It was obviously a difficult decision for him, and I'm glad I persisted.

---

* Theodore Fontane's *Effi Briest* might have been too 'light' for Georg Lindemeyer's taste.

Aunt Bertha has written to say that we should go and celebrate my birthday with them, but unfortunately we won't be able to afford it. At the moment we can't even allow ourselves the smallest trips. Do you remember how delightful it was last year? Our wonderful holiday in the Black Forest? I'm so glad that we were able to do that! The day before yesterday in the evening Hilde and Ruth appeared with a delightful little cactus and some eggnog to wish me all the best for my birthday. It was very sweet of them. Unfortunately I'm not allowed to send you anything at all this year. But I will think of you all even more than usual, if that's at all possible, and I'll hope that Fate will soon deal us a good hand and bring us back together again!

A big hug and kisses from your Mama

25 June 1939
Düsseldorf

GEORG TO EVA-MARIA

Dearest Hen,

Mama was over the moon to get your poem, and it really brightened up her birthday, which was in every respect a harmonious day. Dienstag's address is: Dr Paul Dienstag, Doezastraat 1, Leiden (Holland). But I do strongly urge you not to enter into any discussions or make any requests of him without first consulting me. D. is a complete egotist, and he will only do something for us if he knows he'll get something out of it. You have to be extremely careful when you deal with him, and without knowing it you might complicate or even ruin my literary relationship with him.

The whole situation with Wolfgang is causing me all kinds of worry. He himself writes to say that he thinks he'd be able to pass at Christmas if he had some private tuition. Has the shipment arrived yet?

Kisses from Papa

25 June 1939
Düsseldorf

FRIEDA TO EVA-MARIA
My dearest eldest,

Now the dreaded day is past, but I have to say that everyone did their best to make it as nice as possible for me. Papa especially went to huge efforts to arrange everything with a great deal of loving care. He was already out of bed at 6.30 because he had 'so much to do', as he told me. Aunt Bertha telephoned shortly before eight, still hoping that we might be able to come. Then we had present-giving with cake, our eternal candle and an awful lot of flowers. Papa gave me a charming hatpin and a thin silver chain with little pearls along it, an English dictionary, some chocolate, and a framed photograph of Wolfgang. Now all three of you are hanging up on the wall next to Grandma, opposite where I'm sitting. Erna Böllert did a wonderful job of it. By the way, there's a possibility she might get a job as a photographer in London, but she doesn't yet know whether it will work out. Ruth and her mother were here with Lony yesterday afternoon, and the Hamachers came in the evening. They said they really wanted to spoil me, and they brought along a revolving dish with five sections. They must have spent an awful lot of money on it. Papa says you'd think I was a prima donna, I got that many flowers. The whole apartment is filled with their scent. Aunt Bertha gave me a rubber mat to put in the bath to stop me slipping, and Grandma gave me a bottle of Malaga wine and some chocolates. So you can see that I won't be wasting away. We were so delighted by your little poem. It's quite charming, and your letter too which I read first thing, even before I'd got out of bed. It had already arrived the day before. We all thought of each other so much yesterday that we surely felt it, didn't we, my little girl?

This morning I heard that Aunt Tilly is very ill indeed. I've just asked them whether I should come. I don't particularly want to go anywhere at the moment, for all kinds of reasons, but if I can help in any way at all, then I certainly will.

I've still got lots of letters to write today, so I'll sign off now.

Warm, loving kisses from your Mama

27 June 1939
Düsseldorf

PARENTS TO EVA-MARIA
My dear child,

Your letter with the question you wanted a reply to by today, Tuesday, has just arrived this morning. In any case I'm afraid these are matters you can only resolve yourself. In so far as we are able to judge these things, we definitely both agree that it would be better if you stayed in London, but it's almost impossible to give sound advice from here. If only you could find yourself a room somewhere where you could store all your things. That would really be the best solution.

We haven't heard any more from Wolfgang, and we're dying for his news. I got a card from Frau Heinic on my birthday. The poor woman is now completely on her own; Paul left with a Kindertransport for the north of England on the 20th. Her letter sounded so miserable that we've invited her for lunch on Sunday. At least there are two of us, and we may soon be able to follow you over. For her that's completely out of the question. Her boys are still only at school and can do nothing for her. I'm glad that you were already so independent when you arrived in England. I regularly go along to those sewing lessons, and I've already altered quite a few of my clothes. Gitta always seems pleased to see me, and we get on extremely well. She's still not sure when she'll be able to leave, but I doubt it will be long now. I'm longing to know what you decide about the Cotton thing, and what will happen with Wolfgang!? For his sake it would be good if you were living in London, or at least nearby. I thought that the shippers might have held on to your stuff for a bit longer too. I'm rather worried about the more valuable things.

A big kiss from Mama

Dear Eva-Maria,

Obviously I'm quite against the idea of you moving in with the Cottons. It's hard for us to advise you on how best to turn them down. If Wolfgang comes to London, you could give this as an excuse. If it turns out that you can't get together the money for Ryley's within three months, there's only one thing you can do, and that is to sell something. You'll probably get my card at the same time as this letter.

Loving kisses,

Papa

2 July 1939
Düsseldorf

FRIEDA TO EDITH

My dear child,

Your letter made me very happy – as they so often do – because I always think of how well you must be when you write so cheerfully. You know that I'm constantly pre-occupied by *all* your concerns, and that my thoughts are with the three of you always. – I've now learned how to send pressed flowers properly, and I'll remember that people are so happy to receive them. – I was delighted to see that you still remember the Düsseldorf dialect.

A thousand big kisses from Mama

2 July 1939
Düsseldorf

FRIEDA TO EVA-MARIA

My dearest eldest,

I noticed that you didn't mention a word about Wolf-gang's situation in yesterday's letter. We haven't heard a thing from him all week. I'm assuming you haven't heard anything either, or you would have told us. This endless waiting is so dreadfully nerve-racking! Fräulein Ilse P. went at the beginning of the week to visit the home where she's supposed to be helping out over the summer. The woman who runs it is very unwell so she had to come back again, and I went over to see her. Ilse herself seems really well. She's going to write to Edith as soon as she gets to Uncle Paul's house, and I hope very much that this correspondence will eventually bring about the desired result. It's better that she writes to Edith rather than to you – the letters might be there quicker. I hope it will mean that Edith can have a lovely holiday, and at the very least bring back something nice for you.

I'm not at all sure you'll be able to read my handwriting. I don't feel quite right today and I'm a little jittery. It's nothing to get excited about, but the pharmacist misread the doctor's prescription and gave me the wrong tablets, so I'm a bit confused. It's not that serious, and I'm sure I'll sleep like a log tonight and be back to normal tomorrow. Frau Heinic is coming for lunch today, which isn't exactly going to be a joyous occasion, but we have to do it. I feel so sorry for her.

How nice that you went to the cinema! I'll write more next time. Lony and Ruth send you greetings.

A thousand kisses,
Mama

2 July 1939
Düsseldorf

GEORG TO EVA-MARIA

Dear Eva-Maria,

In my opinion you shouldn't accept the position at the Cottons, whatever happens. You're right in saying that they helped bring you across to England, but this was with the assurance that you would be employed as a companion. If you'd wanted to be a maid, you wouldn't have needed the Cottons, and we certainly wouldn't have sent you over to them on this premise. From here it's hard for me to say how best you could extract yourself from this rather awkward situation. That's something I could assess only with full knowledge of all the relationships involved.

We're very concerned not to have heard a word about Wolfgang's situation, not from either party.

Would you mind telephoning Korth to ask whether he's received my manuscript? He still hasn't confirmed to me that it has arrived, and now I really need to know.

Kisses from Papa

7 July 1939
Düsseldorf

FRIEDA TO EVA-MARIA

My dear child,

I enclose the curriculum vitae you asked for, and I'm also sending you some photographs, even though I'm very loath to part with the one of Papa as it's the last print we have of it. As soon as he gets his new teeth, we're immediately going to have to get a new photograph done.

I rather doubt that I'd still be able to do everything that's required of a housekeeper. After all, I'm already quite run-down, and all the things I've been through have affected me deeply. If you say that I have to be 'as strong as a horse', I can only say that my will is strong, but when it comes to practical achievement I fear I may be a huge disappointment. Besides, everything here is going to take quite a while longer; the house isn't yet sold, and there are a whole lot of other things that need to be sorted out. It's a lot that's being asked of me, and I just don't have it. I can't give you the date of our application as it's not written down here, but as far as I remember we applied in January or February. And by the way, Fräulein Groner wrote to say that there can't be a time limit on the affidavit. She's spoken to Mrs Rosenstein about it.* Now I'm off for my sewing lesson, so I'll write about everything else next time. We received a quite charming letter from Captain Perry today.

By the way, Wolfgang wrote saying that Inter-Aid had asked him where he was going to spend the holidays. The poor boy hasn't a clue what to do.

A thousand kisses,
Mama

---

* These lines refer to an application for permits to leave Germany, made in January or February 1939. Fräulein Groner and Mrs Rosenstein were probably employees of an English refugee organisation.

Frieda Lindemeyer's curriculum vitae

I was born on 24 June 1893 in Berlin, the daughter of Arnold Lewinsky, lawyer and notary, and his wife Hedwig, née Cöhn. I began my schooling in 1899 and graduated in 1909.

I then attended a one-year course in commerce at the Letteverein in Berlin, after which I was employed in my father's office. From the beginning of the war until my marriage in August 1915, I worked voluntarily in a day home for schoolchildren.

From my marriage to Dr Georg Lindemeyer of Elberfeld I have three children: Eva-Maria born in 1917, Edith born in 1919, and Wolfgang born in 1922.

I have always raised my children on my own, and even when they have been seriously ill I have sat up at night with them and cared for them myself under doctor's instructions. I would very much like to work in nursing, in particular as a children's or baby nurse.

I could take on any kind of household work such as cooking etc., and also supervise staff. I could undertake correspondence in German, English or French, and I would also be suited to any kind of public post.

I also have a great deal of experience in handicraft, particularly in knitting clothes, pullovers etc., so I could work as a sales person in a handicraft shop. In fact I am prepared to take on any kind of job that is within my capabilities.

11 July 1939
Düsseldorf

PARENTS TO EVA-MARIA

My dearest eldest,

I definitely think that Papa is right about this, and that it's the only possible solution for you. You'd then be in a position to go off and look for something else, but only if there's still any point in trying to find an office job. You might even be able to fall back on the position in the publishing house, but you'll have to ask Miss King about this first. Do you really think the Cottons will hold it against you if you don't go and work for them? I'm sure they'll understand.

Wolfgang still doesn't know where to go for his holidays. Everyone seems to be going away, and he hasn't heard a thing yet. I wonder what kind of state his other clothes are in if he writes that he urgently needs a suit. What on earth must he look like!

Have you passed on my curriculum vitae? When should I come over? Gitta Glücksmann is leaving on the 20th. What's the latest news of your and Edith's things? Do you need anything else in particular? I'm dying to hear what you're up to, and Edith hasn't written for almost two weeks. I have to get this letter into the post now.

A thousand fat kisses,
Mama

18 July 1939
Düsseldorf

FRIEDA TO EVA-MARIA

My dearest eldest,

Your last letter has just arrived in the second post, together with one from Wolfgang. It's regretful that nothing came of that job, but it may be that the responsibilities you would have had would have been too much anyway. One has to be patient, however hard that may be. Often I have no patience left at all, but this is how things have to be for the moment, and we'll treasure the time when the five of us are together again all the more! Wolfgang says that on 12 August he's going to stay with a parson in Redford, but it's all rather problematic as we don't know what he can do until then (school finishes on 27 or 28 July), let alone what's happening afterwards. If only we could have our boy here for the holidays! It's terribly hard to have to do without all these pleasures. Please promise me you won't spend the little you have saved on a suit for him.

It's wonderful that you spent some time with Edith. By the way, Ilse P. managed to get to her destination the second time round, and yesterday she wrote me a nice card. She doesn't have it at all easy there, but she likes what she's doing and that's the main thing.

Yesterday evening there was a goodbye party for Gitta Glücksmann. She's going off with a Kindertransport on Thursday, and her uncle and aunt from Berlin are going too. I'm sure you'll be hearing from them all soon.

I'm so pleased that Porns is being so friendly and encouraging. If you do some work for him occasionally you can have a bit of practice, and he might then be able to help you later on too. It's terribly funny that you bumped into Dr Bondi – that must have been a nice surprise. Are things working out for him over there? I do hope so. I'm sorry that Gitta is leaving us. She's such a lovely, gregarious thing, and sadly the only youthful element around to cheer us all up. It's a terrible blow for her father, who's so ill.

Should we write to the Casswells at some point? To thank them? It's lovely that you've become so friendly with them. So, that's enough for today! I've still got to write to Wolfgang.

Kisses from Mama

21 July 1939
Düsseldorf

FRIEDA TO EVA-MARIA
My dear child,

Your very sweet letter has just arrived! Well, there again we were supposed to reply by Friday, i.e. today, and your letter only arrived in the second post. So no hope of an answer by Friday! Wolfgang is going to stay with a parson in Redford from the 12 August onwards, and I think that's all been confirmed already. It may be that he could go and stay with the Cottons until the 12th, but I'm sure it would be awfully boring being alone there with Miss Cotton – no fun at all for a little lad like him. If only we knew now what's going to happen to him after the holidays! All this uncertainty and inertia is enough to drive you to despair. It's so depressing that nothing came of Mrs Mejnen's discussions. I was delighted at the idea of you finally being able to store all your things in your own room – in fact I was rather counting on it. Haven't you spoken to the man at the publishing house yet? I'll write to the Casswells sometime in the next few days. I'm just not in the mood at the moment. I'm going to try to get permission to replenish Wolfgang and Edith's old and worn-out clothes, dresses and suits. The children must have something to wear. I don't know whether it'll be possible, but I'll certainly give it a try. – The Wimbledon Committee have managed to accommodate Gitta G. with a family in Wimbledon. Have you heard of that committee? I'll try to find out the address for you this afternoon at my sewing class, so you can send Gitta's letter there.

A thousand kisses,

Mama

PS Try to find out the telephone number of this lady and call her about Gitta's address: Mrs Mathilde Freund, 116a Durham Road, London SW20. But do it soon.

25 July 1939
Düsseldorf

PARENTS TO EVA-MARIA

My dear child,

I was terribly happy when I heard that you had visited Wolfgang, and so you've seen both of my little ones recently. How did he look? Has he changed very much? At the end of this week it will be a whole year since he was here for the holidays! It would be so lovely if I had that to look forward to again this year!

I have very mixed feelings about Wolfgang attending another school until Christmas. I'm sure it could be advantageous to his future, but all that slog before Christmas is definitely a little harsh. If only we could be sure that he would pass then. What does Wolfgang have to say about all this? That's the most important thing, after all. We didn't get any post from him today. Of course it would be best of all if you and Wolfgang could live together some time soon. Then you'd all have a real home!

Papa went to the foreign exchange office yesterday to enquire about Wolfgang's suit and clothes for him and Edith. They said we should make an application, but of course no one seemed to know whether or not it would be accepted.

Has Dr Bondi been in touch with you yet? He wanted to let you know that a Dr Ruhemann (a doctor from Berlin) might be able to help with your job situation. If you haven't yet heard from him, you should telephone. His address is Dr Fritz Bondi, 21 Sussex Gardens. He very much wants to be able to help you out. – Have you spoken to Gitta? Have you not yet heard of any job possibilities for me? If necessary I could of course come over to meet any prospective employers. We might be going to Berlin after all. There's nowhere else for us to go, and in the end what we really need is a change of scene.

I'm getting a new cleaning lady on Tuesday. Old Dornbusch has really gone off the rails. Who can tell whether the new one will be any better?! I'm so looking forward to reading your next letter.

A thousand kisses,
Mama

Dear child,

Let's hope everything works out for Wolfgang. I've just got my dentures and 'bared my teeth' (so to speak) at the Hamachers when they were here just now.

Loving kisses,

Papa

28 July 1939
Düsseldorf

PARENTS TO EDITH

My dear girl,

One year ago today, at exactly this time, we called you on the telephone to give you the good news that you could come over and see us, and Wolfgang had already been here since the day before. I live with the memories of those three weeks when we were all together and could even spend our special day on 5 August with you all. I hope with all my heart that we will be together again soon; perhaps a year from now we'll even be able to celebrate our silver wedding anniversary with our children.

I don't know if you've already heard that Wolfgang will be attending a different school in Oxfordshire after the holidays, and he's to take his exams at Christmas. There's nothing at all we can do about it from here, and we'll just have to accept it, although I scarcely believe that he'll be able to pass by then. Your holidays seem to be very late in the year, and I hope the weather is still good enough for you to be able to enjoy them. I'll see what I can do about your clothes. I agree that you need one of those grey slip-ons, and shoes too. But you'll still have to let me know whether you want heels or not, and roughly what shape (sporty, for example?). Maybe you should draw me a little picture. I think you're a size 40, but have a look on the soles or inside to see if there's a number. When I've looked around I can put in an application with the prices, and I'll only buy them when it's been approved so that we don't have to pay double for too many things at this end. I'm almost certain you won't be able to have them for your holidays, but I should be able to get them to you in September.

Warm sweet kisses from Mama

Dear child,

I'm delighted that your trip to Paris will definitely be going ahead. There you'll see the world from a completely different angle, and whatever happens you'll learn to understand England even better just by being able to compare one country with the other. I'll write more about all this before you leave.

Warmest kisses from Papa

29 July 1939
Düsseldorf

PARENTS TO EVA-MARIA
My dearest eldest,

Your lovely letter has just arrived. It's just wonderful that you're going to be able to see Wolfgang again so soon. When I've finished this letter, I'll finally force myself to write to the Casswells. They're obviously quite splendid people, and it's such a stroke of luck that you've got to know them. But tell me now: wouldn't it be a better idea if you took a job in housekeeping first, just to get a start in it? From what I hear it would be completely impossible for you to change your permit until you've been working in house-keeping for at least a year. The longer you put it off, the longer it will be before that year comes to an end. So do give this some very careful thought. Just think how nice it would be if we could both work in the same household!

We still haven't decided when we'll be going to Berlin, or whether we'll go at all. Papa still has all kinds of problems with his teeth, so we will have to wait for them to be resolved anyway. And you know that it doesn't do my nerves any good at all when Papa stays there too: that small apartment with one room already rented out, and Papa in the dining room on the leather sofa! He can't go for a good walk from there either. On the other hand it's completely out of the question to rent another room for him further out of town, even though that would probably be the best solution. I don't particularly feel like going either. It'd be a different matter if you were there too, and we could go on nice little outings together, but like this?

Over the past few days I've been thinking so much about this time last year, when Wolfgang had just arrived and we were looking forward to seeing Edith. Let's only hope that this won't be just a memory, but part of the future too! We simply *have* to be together for our silver wedding anniversary next year.

A thousand fat kisses, Mama
Loving kisses from Papa

1 August 1939
Düsseldorf

PARENTS TO WOLFGANG

My dear Wolfgang,

We've just received your lovely card, after we'd waited for a letter from you for the whole of last week. These short cards are all very well, but they never tell us what we're most interested to hear. It's wonderful that you can go back to Chute, and I hope the weather is better this time! And how lovely that Eva-Maria will be coming to see you tomorrow! Your school report is very respectable except for a few minor points. Papa is making a copy of it now to send back to you. Now we're both hoping for a longer letter from you, and then we'll write more. We might be going to Berlin soon.

A fat kiss from Mama
Very best wishes, Papa

6 August 1939
Düsseldorf

FRIEDA TO EVA-MARIA

My dear child,

Your letter of yesterday gave us so much joy, particularly the pretty poem with the flowers on it. But I'm still glad the day has passed for another year – it's on days like those that I notice what I am missing twice as much. Let's hope with all our hearts that next year we'll be able to celebrate our silver wedding anniversary all together, happily and in good health. But who knows what trials we may still have to face! – We may be going to Berlin on Friday, or only a few days later. Papa will be coming with me as far as Kreiensen, and then he's going to make a little detour to Göttingen, where there are various negotiations going on to do with the sale of the house. The son of an estate agent there came to see us here on Friday, and gave us all kinds of news, for example that Leibholz is probably going to be moving to Berlin. Have you seen them at all?

I'm assuming your purse is still rather understocked since you didn't write to us at all last week. It's awful not to be able to do anything to help; and I can't even get you reply coupons any more. We'll wait patiently for another week to go by, until you can write us a long letter, and we will look forward to it.

It's all very well what you write about Wolfgang, but not one of his letters has any kind of personal content and there's never a loving word. It's all just duty. I'm sure you can understand how sad that sometimes makes me feel. He hasn't written anything about the plans for him after the holidays, and he knows how much we're interested in every little detail. I'll wait now until after our trip before I sort out some clothes for him, and then I'll apply for the authorisation. In the sales I bought Edith a beautiful coat for the autumn. I'm sure she would have loved to have it for her holidays, but I can't see how that would have worked out.

Your news of Dr Ruhemann is not at all reassuring. After Frau Bondi's descriptions I had very much set my hopes on him. She told me he was the most selfless, helpful person you could hope to meet, and that he would really be capable of doing something. Now the whole thing makes me feel less than comfortable. They will have heard from their son (who, by the way, is an extremely talented and intelligent young man) how things stand between you and Dr Ruhemann, and of course they'll describe the whole situation as he perceives it. So the Glücksmanns will get a less than favourable impression of you, and I find this really embarrassing as I often spend time with them at my sewing lessons. Well, there's nothing we can do about it now. If only that relief programme for lawyers which Demuth talked about would soon become a reality!* That could certainly do us some good.

Yes, I certainly am keen on you getting yourself a housekeeping job after all this time. You've got to start somewhere, and the Perrys won't be able to keep you on for ever. In the end everyone will think that you don't *want* to work. I had somehow persuaded myself you would be telling me in yesterday's letter that you had got a job, but now I'll just have to keep on waiting and hoping.

Warmest kisses from Mama

6 August 1939
Düsseldorf

GEORG TO EVA-MARIA

My dear child,

Many, many thanks for your dear letter, which showed such profound sensitivity! We hope so much that all your wishes come true. But for the time being it looks rather

---

* No further detail could be established about a relief programme for lawyers.

unfavourable in this respect: 'The Day of Judgement' has been rejected by Fox and other film companies, and Fox have also turned down 'Aziz and Azizah'. Mr Bassler, the director of Fox's London office, wrote about the latter: 'This Arabian Nights story is not the kind of material Mr Zannek is looking for. However, I am glad to have had the opportunity to read it.' By the way, Zannek is head of the German section at Fox in Hollywood, to whom Bassler also sent 'The Day of Judgement'.

I'm enclosing with this letter a copy of Wolfgang's school report. Perhaps you could make another copy from this not particularly neat version and pass it on to Miss Barshall. We were very pleased with the report as it seems that he is showing an obvious talent for the sciences. But it's true that there are also some rather less favourable comments. As far as Dr R. is concerned, I think you behaved quite properly. I no longer have the slightest confidence in him after the ridiculous role he played in drawing up the Cyprus plan. It's best that you ignore him completely.

Loving kisses,
Papa

11 August 1939
Düsseldorf

PARENTS TO EVA-MARIA
My dear child,

We're off first thing tomorrow, so I'm sure you can imagine how little time I have to write letters. But since you urgently needed an answer by airmail, I'm just going to say the following: it is possible that you offended Dr Ruhemann with your behaviour all the same. I cannot judge from here whether he actually means well by you, and really wants to help. All I know is that here he's more or less described as a supernaturally good and helpful individual who seems to have been a great support to Bondi. I think that you've now got to write to him saying that you never intended to give offence or behave badly towards him, but that if in your desire to get ahead you have somehow hurt his feelings, then you are extremely sorry. You'll have to tell him that it would have been impossible for you to be entirely at his disposal due to your great commitment towards the Perrys. Anyway, you wouldn't have been able to raise the necessary expenses, as when you're not living with the Perrys you have to subsist on charity. As for the teaching, first of all it's not going to be much help to you if you earn no more than you'd spend on fares, and secondly you might then have to worry about causing problems with the whole permit business.

That's more or less what I think. To be able to give you really good advice, I'd have to know the man. I can well believe that my little girl, whose behaviour is otherwise good, may sometimes have a certain manner that might surprise people who don't know her better, and could even offend someone who is trying to be helpful. I'm not claiming that's how it was in this particular case. If he asks how he might be able to help you, it seems fairly obvious and the possibilities are endless. – Anyway, that's enough for now. I just wish I could help you more, spiritually and otherwise! I very much hope that I've been able to do at least something for you with these few short lines. Send some good news to Berlin!

A thousand kisses,
Mama

Dear Hen,

I would actually suggest that you're rather more brusque in your answer to Dr R., since he's shown himself to be a rather undistinguished individual (as well as a complete idiot). But you'd better do what Mama says so that we don't make too much of a bad impression here with the Glücksmanns, and be sure to avoid Dr R. in future. He's not going to be able to do anything for you anyway.

Loving kisses,
Papa

17 August 1939
Berlin

FRIEDA TO WOLFGANG
My dear boy,

Now you've arrived in Redford, where with any luck you'll have a jolly nice time. In your next letter do tell us about everything you're experiencing, what sort of people you're spending your time with, how you're spending the time, and roughly where Redford is in England, whether in the South or North or wherever.

I was so happy to hear that you'd once again had a nice time in Chute. They must be splendid people. And then at the end you spent some days in London! That must have been wonderful, seeing the two girls again! How do the two of them look now? Have they put on a bit of weight, and do they look fresh and healthy? I do hope I'll get a little card from the three of you tomorrow morning. I'm sure you thought just a little bit about us when you were all together.

Papa has been in Göttingen and arrived here on Tuesday evening. Today he went off to a suburb where we've rented a room for him for a couple of weeks. It's rather cramped here in the apartment, and he'll be able to have a better rest out there where it's greener. I've been here since Saturday night, and I do so hope to have a good rest myself. I certainly need one after all the things we've been through in the past year. A letter from Peter arrived today. It was fascinating: he wrote all about the things he's experiencing, and about the conditions in that country. I could really picture everything. Let's hope you'll learn to write better letters soon – then we might actually be able discover a little bit about your own life, and not just what goes on around you. I suppose that will probably come with time, at least that's what I always hope.

Farewell for today, my child. I hope you have a really lovely holiday, and I send you one thousand fat kisses,

Mama

26 August 1939
Berlin

GEORG TO EVA-MARIA

Dear child,

Here follows the German text of a letter of application, and I'm sending back the advertisements too. With the current international situation I can hardly hope for success, and certainly not from the first post advertised. The second advertisement is obviously aimed at Germans living in England. We're very relieved that Edith is now back home. Better safe than sorry. Frau Leibholz wrote to me today saying that she'd very much like to see you. Do go and see her as soon as you can. I'm enclosing two sheets with my signature.

In haste, with many kisses,
your Papa

Letter of application

With reference to your advertisement in issue number . . . of (name of newspaper), I am writing to apply for the position. I am 52 years old, a doctor of law, and I worked for 18 years as a lawyer at the regional court in Düsseldorf. In 1933 I was forced to give up my profession because of the race laws. Since then I have occupied myself largely by writing scripts for films on both literary and legal themes. On the literary side I wrote a film comedy which received widespread recognition, but it could not be developed by the production company because they got into financial

difficulties. I have also read widely in other fields of literature, and I possess a fairly broad knowledge of European
writers. On the legal side, I have had essays published in
various specialist periodicals, some of which have been on
the subject of film rights. I would be grateful if you could
consider my application.

*In August 1939 the international situation was once again
becoming increasingly tense. Edith had gone to France to
visit Frieda's brother Paul, but returned to England earlier
than planned.*

28 *August 1939*
Berlin

FRIEDA TO EVA-MARIA
My dearest eldest,

Now everything is once again in the utmost confusion.
Pray God that the worst can be averted! I'm just glad to be
here with all this dreadful anxiety and upheaval, rather than
sitting at home on my own. Uncle Paul's telegram arrived at
11.30 at night, and we immediately sent another in reply. At
5.30 the next morning I telephoned Uncle Paul's house,
hoping at least to be able to hear Edith's voice, but she had
already left. From what I gather, that's probably the best
thing she could have done. I only wish I knew that she'd
arrived safely back in Horam. I hope we get post from her
tonight. Whatever happens you must all write as often as
you can, because who knows for how long that will still be

possible. – By now you'll have received Papa's application letter. I'm afraid you're going to have to enclose a couple of stamps out of your few shillings. We can't get any here, and they've asked for them. – I think these highly desirable positions might have long since been filled though.

As far as Inter-Aid is concerned, it's probably best that you keep in touch with them so that we'll be able to find out what's going to happen with our boy. I'm so glad that you're not too far apart from each other – I should really count myself lucky.

So, my good child, we must put our trust in everything we know, and have faith that a kindly hand will protect us from the worst – as so often before.

I send you a very big hug and a thousand kisses,

Mama

29 August 1939
Berlin

FRIEDA TO EDITH, EVA-MARIA AND WOLFGANG
My dear good girl,

I can't tell you how happy I was to read your dear lines after this dreadfully long wait, and to know that you'd got back home safely. The telegram arrived here at 11.30 on Thursday night. You can imagine what a fright we got, because at that time we had no idea that the situation had got so serious. Even though it's lovely that you had those three days there, I'm so desperately sorry that you spent all your precious money in vain. We haven't had any post from Eva-Maria for about eight days, and she hasn't answered any of my pressing

questions. I just have to assume that one of the letters has gone
astray, which wouldn't surprise me, what with everything
being as it is at the moment. You know how worried we get if
we don't hear from you, which is why I'm asking you all to
write as often as you can while it's still possible. This part of
the letter was just for you. What follows here is meant for all
three of you, as I don't know whether we'll still be able to
write to you after today. Whatever happens, you shouldn't be
afraid for us. We will stay here for the moment, at least until
we are a bit clearer about what's going to happen, and I am
glad to be together with Aunt Bertha at this worrying time.
Remember that we are always in God's hands, and we cannot
give up hope now. There is always the possibility that reason
will prevail at the last minute, and we will all be spared the
worst. But if there comes a time when we can't keep in touch
with each other, we will just have to come to terms with that
too. We must never forget that His merciful hand has
protected us from the worst many times already. You will
still always have one another, and you're not too far apart.
For that alone we have kindly Providence to thank, as all
uncertainty and worry is so much easier to bear when you can
share it with each other. I want you to know that whatever
happens we will try anything to remain in contact with you
through letters, so please write to us too, even just to let us
know that you are well. I do hope we will still hear what is
going to be happening with our boy; where he's going to be at
school next term, and what his future will hold. Will you, my
dear little Edith, achieve the success you are hoping for with
your career, and my dearest eldest, will you find a job that is
reasonably promising and carve out your future from there?

My dearly beloved three, let's keep on hoping with all our might, and never allow ourselves to be defeated!

Loving kisses to you all, from your Mama

2 September 1939
Berlin

PARENTS TO EVA-MARIA
My dear child,

We were so delighted to receive post from you today, and pray that it will continue to be possible for us to hear from each other. – It's wonderful that you've just started a new job. Did you get the first letter we sent to Redhill?* Let's hope that your first impressions are well founded, and that you will be extremely happy there. It's not right at all that you're being so spoilt, but on the other hand if you're performing your duties well, I suppose we'll let it pass this time! Please write and let us know about the work you're doing there, and what you're up to otherwise!

We also got a letter from Wolfgang today. What on earth will become of him now! All this uncertainty is ghastly. You didn't say whether you'd heard anything else from Inter-Aid. At some point those people really have to decide what they intend for him. I hope they'll also understand that it's now going to be quite impossible for us to provide him with any more clothes etc., and that they'll have to see to it that the poor child doesn't go around looking too ragged.

---

* From September 1939, Eva-Maria was employed as a secretary at a Christian organisation in Redhill, Surrey.

It's wonderful that Edith is now at the seaside. We haven't heard any more from her since she sent a card saying she'd arrived back safely. – I'd like to write to the Haffendens, and also to the Perrys, to thank them again for everything they've done, but with the best will in the world I really don't have the concentration just now to compose an even halfway intelligible letter in English. Please tell this to Edith – I'm sure everyone there will understand.

Yesterday we got a reply from London saying that they were considering Papa's letter of application. I wonder whether you could follow it up some time; we can't do anything at all from here, although at this stage I'm not sure there's any point, to be honest. We have to hope with all our hearts that this dreadful period will soon come to an end, and that peace will return. Keep your spirits up, my dear girl, and think as often and as lovingly of us as we think of you all.

A thousand kisses,
Mama

Dear Lady Stussfield!

We were delighted to receive your letter. I hope very much that life at your institute continues to be as positive as it was when you started there. I'm sure we will find a way of keeping in touch with each other.

Warm kisses,
Papa

2 September 1939
Berlin

PARENTS TO WOLFGANG

My good boy,

I am so relieved to have had a letter from you today, especially as it reports that you've also had post from us. As long as I know that the three of you are well, I am content, and I can cope with everything else. I wish we could foretell what our future holds! I'm sure you know by now that Eva-Maria has got a job, which she's already started. The letter we got from her today sounded very content, and I do hope that she'll continue to be happy there. She also wrote to say that Edith is at the seaside, still enjoying a good holiday.

You might as well continue to write to me here; I doubt we'll be going anywhere for the time being, and it's probably a good thing that we're not sitting around at home on our own. It would be better if the apartment here weren't so small, but it's quite manageable and I'm glad we can all be together.

So, my little lad, please write again soon. We'll keep on trying to get letters through to you. Just keep your chin up, and everything will be fine.

Warmest kisses,
Mama

My dear boy,

I was also delighted to get your letter. We hope to find ways of getting letters through to you even if developments continue to close up all the channels, which is what appears

to be happening now. All of this will come to an end, and I
don't think that it will be long now. Of course what we
want most of all is news of what's happening to you next
term.

Kisses from Papa

*With the official declaration of war on 3 September 1939,
communication between Georg and Frieda Lindemeyer and
their children obviously became more difficult; they could
not send letters as frequently, and they were obliged to find
alternative means of keeping in touch with one another,
sometimes using intermediaries and ultimately relying on
the short messages which could be transmitted via the Red
Cross. Often it was some months before they were able to
discover their children's whereabouts.*

13 September 1939
Amsterdam

PAUL DIENSTAG TO EVA-MARIA

Dear Miss Lindemeyer,

Your father has just written to me from Germany, from
Berlin in fact. From the information given in his letter I am
able to tell you the following:

Your parents and relatives in Berlin are well, and your
father tells me that life goes on more or less as normal. Your
parents intend to stay in Berlin for the time being, to see
how the situation develops, and then to return to Düsseldorf. Your parents are in good health, and hope you and

your siblings are too. If at all possible, your father asks that you get a message to him by any means appropriate saying how you are, and where, and to write to the address in Berlin for the moment. It would probably be best if you sent your letter here, and I could pass it on to your father. I don't know the address in Berlin, however, so you would have to send that to me too. Please pass this letter on to your siblings.

With best regards,
P. Dienstag
Chief Editor of the periodical 'Geistiges Eigentum'

21 October 1939
Düsseldorf

PARENTS TO EDITH, EVA-MARIA AND WOLFGANG
[incomplete]

My beloved children,

Your letters arrived here yesterday – it was the first joyful day we've had in a long time. I am so happy and thankful to have heard from you at last, and to know that you're all well. But there was nothing from you, my dear little Edith. Why was that? Is there something the matter? I very much hope that I will soon get a letter from you too. Of course now it will take much longer for us to hear from one another, but provided we know that news is on its way, then the wait becomes easier.

And what about you, my big little boy! You'll see that there's a place in life for you too. It's simply wonderful, and so comforting for us, that Fate has led you to such good and generous people.* Make sure you always work hard, and demonstrate your gratitude, your unceasing application and your energy to all those people who are supporting you. It's too lovely that you've been lucky enough to end up in a house like that. Even if you don't manage to find yourself an apprenticeship immediately, it won't do you any harm at all to spend a bit of time working in the joinery; it will certainly improve your manual dexterity. Whatever happens, I have complete confidence in all three of you, and I'm sure you will fulfil the roles that this life has destined for you.

We've been back here since the end of September, and we've let two rooms to an elderly couple until 1 November. We're somehow managing to get by. We five cannot and will not let our courage diminish, and we must make sure that we remain strong. I send you three a big, big hug and an infinite number of kisses, and very best wishes from everyone who knows you – Hilde, Ruth, Lony, the Hamachers, from the Pastor and his wife and everyone else too.

My dear ones,

That was the greatest happiness for us, when your news arrived here! And today, via Ilse, we even heard the next instalment! I don't think we need to worry about you three at all. What has been decided for Wolfgang is definitely the best solution. The house is not yet sold, which is why we're

_____

* For a period from September 1939 onwards, Wolfgang lived at Doddington Hall, Lincolnshire, and worked in a joinery before beginning an engineering course at a technical school in Lincoln.

rather restricted financially, but we can get by well enough with the money we're receiving in rent. I'm helping out a little with the housekeeping, and apart from that I'm continuing with my work as before. I think I'm making good progress. All our friends send their regards. We'll all just have to sit tight until things improve. If we all keep our chins up, we'll be fine.

23 October 1939
Düsseldorf

FRIEDA TO EDITH, EVA-MARIA AND WOLFGANG

My dearest three,

Ilse Peters has just forwarded me the letter you wrote to her, my dear eldest. I am so overjoyed to hear from you all, and to know that you are well and going about your respective work. Have you already had permission to stay on in that job? I'd so like to know! What's the matter with your boss? Is she very ill, or will she soon be able to get back to her job and allow you to get on with the work you're supposed to be doing? What a shame, my little Edith, that you weren't able to spend the rest of your holiday with Eva-Maria, as you'd both planned. But if you were needed back at work, there's nothing you could have done about it. You've only got another two months of training, and then everything will start to improve for you too. I wonder whether you'll still be able to let me know when you've got yourself a job, and what it is you'll be doing. Did you get the coat? What are Grete and Ellen up to, by the way? Do you ever see them?

And now to you, my boy! I am so happy that you can be there, and that there are people who want to help you choose a career. I would so love to see how much you've grown. You might be even taller than your Mama by now, and maybe I wouldn't even recognise you any more (although I think I probably would)! I hope you're not being so spoiled by your foster-parents that you wouldn't be able to get used to life with us again. What on earth must your suits and clothes look like by now? Just remember one thing, my son: work as hard as you can and you will succeed, and never forget to show your gratitude!

My dearest children, I hope very much that we'll have good news from you all again soon. Never forget what we have experienced so often: when our need is greatest, God's help is close at hand. All five of us are living only for the same purpose, which we can all envisage, and that is what we always have to look forward to. I embrace you and kiss you!

Frieda

1940

PARENTS AND RUTH SCHOEN TO EVA-MARIA

My dearest eldest,

This letter is meant mainly for you alone, but you may pass snippets of it on to the others. I'm sure you'll have received Dienstag's letter by now. What about sending a reply via Ilse's friend? More than anything else I long to hear about Edith's job possibilities, and whether Wolfgang has already begun his apprenticeship. The fact that I haven't had a note from Wolfgang himself since November makes me extremely anxious – I hope that something comes soon. This is the one and only thing that we still have to look forward to. I am eternally grateful to Ruth's boss for everything that he's still doing for us. There are still some good people in this world. Ruth herself is absolutely charming, as I've often said before. She comes to visit us faithfully every single week, and she's so lovely with me that when we're together I quite often forget that we're not related. Today she's coming for lunch, and we're having steamed dumplings!

But now to the main reason for this letter: please could you write as soon as possible to Fräulein Sponer – it's such a difficult and long-winded process from here. Apparently if you're getting your affidavit from friends rather than relatives, you need two, in which case we won't get anywhere with ours. But they've been going through much quicker recently so we really have to make sure in good time that the one we've got is adequate. And please also ask her – on the basis of her experience in England – what she imagines we might be able to do when we're over there. Could I get a job in housekeeping, or what else would she advise me to do, and could Georg make a living there as a freelance writer (on patent law etc.), and perhaps also do some teaching? We really must be clear on all this so that we're not a burden to anyone when we're there. Something really must happen soon!

Our tenants are about to leave so we're trying to find some replacements. It seems to be almost impossible, even though we've advertised etc. – there are simply not enough people left here now.* There's so much I want to know about you all, but all the news we get is so inadequate. I just wish it were peacetime again! It's so incredibly cold here that I rarely go outside. I'm so glad you have all those warm things, because I'm sure the weather is no different where you are. Please write me a long letter soon! Give each of the others a big fat kiss from me, and save one for yourself, or lots even.

---

* As 'non-Aryans', the Lindemeyers were allowed to have only Jews or Christians of Jewish origin renting rooms in their apartment.

Dear girl,

You will have learned everything worth knowing from the lines you've just read. Of myself, I can only tell you what I've already said in previous letters. I'm enjoying my work and getting on well with it. We are healthy and in good spirits. The same can be said of all our friends and relatives. We see the Hamachers and the Glücksmanns almost every week. Please make sure that Wolfgang writes as soon as possible.

Warmest wishes from your Papa, the old peasant

Dear Eva-Maria,

And here are a few short lines from me. Your dear parents are well, although they're rather worried not to have heard from Wolfgang directly. Please see what you might be able to do on that front. Here we have no way of knowing the reason for his silence! I'm quite well, as before. I've still got plenty of work to do, and for the time being that has to be my priority. I'm afraid I can't think of anything particularly jolly to tell you.

Today's lunch was absolutely delicious! We had steamed dumplings with vanilla sauce. I've eaten so much I think I might explode. I hope you're extremely well and cheerful, and that the weather over there isn't freezing cold, as it is here. I'm keeping all my fingers crossed that things soon work out for us all, and I send you my very best wishes. Please also give my regards to the other two.

[Ruth]

21 March 1940
Düsseldorf

PARENTS TO EVA-MARIA, EDITH AND WOLFGANG

My beloved three,

It so happens that Ruth's boss is going off for his Easter holidays tomorrow, so I can send you all a sign of life today, on your birthday, my dearest eldest. It's the first time you've been apart from us on your birthday, and I wish I could be sure that you're being brave and not too sad! Ruth is coming over for lunch, and the talk will be only of you. I have not had a word from any of you for such an awfully long time – more than five weeks – so you can imagine just how worried I am. Each day I long for post from you, but sadly I'm disappointed every time, until finally one day a letter does actually arrive. If only that day were today! I wonder whether you did get that job closer to Eva-Maria, my little Edith? And what about you, my boy! It would be just awful if you were still sitting around doing absolutely nothing. How are you keeping yourself busy? Can't you go back to those other people? I still don't know why you left – I hope nothing unpleasant happened.

This Sunday it's Easter, and I hope so much that you all have a lovely holiday! Do you remember how you all used to hunt for eggs, and Papa could never find any? Let's look forward to doing all these things again some time. All I hope for now is that a lengthy letter will arrive here very soon indeed, and that in it I will discover everything I want to know about you and your lives. Now I hold each of you in my arms and hug you tight, one after the other!

My three dear children,

On the occasion of your birthday, my dear 'old' thing, we've got a bottle of very nice wine which we'll be drinking together with your friend at lunchtime. We'll be thinking of you all day long, and hoping that we'll be able to find each other in good health very soon. There's really not very much else to report. I can of course understand why we have not heard from you for so long, but we are desperate for a letter none the less. I hope the three of you have a truly lovely Easter holiday.

With warmest wishes
from your Papa, the old peasant

24 April 1940
London

WOLFGANG TO HIS PARENTS
Dear Uncle Toni,*

Many thanks for your lovely letter. I've finally found a job, which I've already started. I'm working in an enormous department store in one of the best areas of London. My job is to deal with all the orders for woollens, or the ones that come through the post anyway. It's all rather basic, and I hope I'll be able to get something else soon (at the same store). I work from 8.55 in the morning until 18.10, with an hour off for lunch and half an hour for coffee. I don't have to work on Saturday afternoons, but then I get dreadfully bored.

---

* Wolfgang used this pseudonym to hide his parents' identity from the Nazis. This letter was probably sent via an intermediary, a friend of Frieda's living in Switzerland.

How are you? I am quite well, so you needn't worry about me.

The place I'm living in at the moment is not particularly nice, but I hope to find something better before long. I'm looking forward to meeting up with Eva-Maria and Edith soon. They're not living at all far from here. I must close now, dear Uncle Toni.

Very many best wishes from Wolfgang

27 August 1940
Düsseldorf

PARENTS TO WOLFGANG [communication via the Red Cross] Happy about news. Where's Edith? Receive monthly Red Cross letters? Please all write. Eva-Maria brave? Work possibilities? We're at home, well. Thousand kisses all three!

1941—47

2 February 1941
Düsseldorf

PARENTS TO EVA-MARIA

My dearly beloved child,

When Papa brought your letter up to me this Sunday morning, it was the most wonderful moment we'd had for a long, long time. Even if its contents have long been overtaken by events – it's dated 11 November – I was still so happy and thankful to have a sign of life from you at last. But if you've been there since May I don't understand why you didn't write sooner.* Lots of people have been receiving post from internees. Gitta wrote too, but that's quite some time ago now. I haven't heard a thing from Wolfgang since the beginning of July. I would just love to know where he is, whether he's learning anything at all, and how his health is, particularly his kidneys. It's a huge relief that Edith was able to stay on in her job. I hope that's still the case, and that nothing has changed in the meantime. Her last Red Cross

---

* Since May 1940 Eva-Maria had been interned as an 'enemy alien' on the Isle of Man, where she met a few of her old friends from Düsseldorf, including Gitta Glücksmann.

communication was sent at the beginning of September. Are you able to keep in touch with the two of them?

It makes me so happy to think that you're there with kind people, and I'm sure Marianne's mother is a great support to you, both practically and morally. Do give her my regards, even though she doesn't know me. I'm very glad that you're learning the violin, and I can picture how lovely it will be at home in the future, with you playing the violin and the other two at the piano. Maybe I should start practising again too! What will you be able to do when you're released? I'm assuming that you won't be able to go back to Redhill. Grandma is in very good health. I went to see her on Thursday, and I was amazed at how well she still looks at eighty. News from Aunt Bertha is also good, although sadly they haven't heard anything from Peter for a year and a half, and nobody knows where Günther is either.

Unfortunately your letter didn't arrive in time for Christmas, as you'd hoped, but I still managed to decorate a tiny tree for Papa. Hilde was here on Christmas Eve, and Ruth came to see us a few days before. Both of them continue to be loyal souls. I'm going to write this letter on my own and use up every bit of space, and Papa will write as well, the day after tomorrow, in the hope that at least one of our letters will get to you. We must all try to get through this difficult period of separation, and keep on looking forward to a not-too-distant, joyful reunion!

It's a good thing that you have so many duties, and that you find your work satisfying – I expect this will keep your spirits up and help you see this whole thing through. I'm particularly glad that Grete is not so far from you. Give her our very best wishes. So where is Ellen? I hope this letter will reach you in time for your birthday, my dear girl. I send you my very best wishes, my child, and hope that they are at least partly fulfilled! If you can write to the others, please pass on an infinite number of kisses. All I think about, day and night, is you three. I embrace you and kiss you, my love.

Your Mama

A thousand kisses, my beloved child, from your Papa

4 February 1941
Düsseldorf

GEORG TO EVA-MARIA
My beloved child,

The day before yesterday, when your letter arrived, was one of the best days of my life. We had looked forward to it so fervently, and yet it took so many months to arrive! Mama wrote to you two days ago, and I am writing again today in the hope that at least one of our letters will get to you. I am repeating a few of the things Mama has said just in case one of the letters gets lost. Don't be annoyed that I've typed this letter: I am now so unused to longhand that my writing is becoming quite illegible, and I use up far too much space.

Mama and I are quite well and in good health, Grandma too. Mama visited her only five days ago. Aunt Bertha and Uncle Josef are both well. I sent copies of your letter to all of them. We are still living in our old apartment, which is unchanged and exactly as it was when you were still here. – We celebrated Christmas extremely well, and we even had a little tree. It goes without saying that we spent the whole time thinking of you all.

What you write about your life over there is reassuring, and even most interesting. I hope that you're being well looked after. You may have been released by now, in which case we hope that we'll soon have news via the Red Cross of your whereabouts, how you are and what you're up to. We were so proud when we read that you had been made the house representative – of course your election to this position proves that people both respect you and have confidence in you. In this function you will learn a great deal that will be of use to you in later life: you will develop an ability to judge character; you will have to think independently and responsibly; and you will have to negotiate. You may even make contacts here and there. And of course I am particularly proud that you are attending talks on historical topics – you are your father's daughter after all! Whether it's possible now or only after your release, please make sure that you get to read Trevelyan's 'History of England'. It's a complete masterpiece, and I'm quite sure there will by now be a second edition of the German translation. And you're even learning to play the violin! Even if you are only able to learn the rudiments in your current circumstances, at least you have taken the first step, and I'm sure that means you'll pick it up again later on. It did me such a lot of good to read that you have been so responsive to my work. I'm still working on the same thing as when you left. I am actually now getting to the end of it, but it will still take me a considerable time. A while ago I also finished a substantial new legal treatise, and this too has been accepted for publication by 'Geistiges Eigentum', even thought its scope goes far beyond the framework of the journal. It is still unclear when or whether the next issue of the journal is due to appear.

Ruth came straight from work to hear your news. In fact everybody is absolutely delighted by your letter, and they all send their regards. So write again soon, my beloved child.

                    With warm kisses from your Papa

                                        21 March 1941
                                        Düsseldorf

PARENTS TO EVA-MARIA
My dearly beloved child,

Your Red Cross message from 19 November arrived to-day, on your birthday, in answer to ours of 5 August. I was simply overjoyed to hear from you on this special day, today of all days when I am thinking of you all the time, every single hour! I wonder where on earth you are. I am writing to the address you've given without knowing whether you'll receive these lines there, or if you'll read them at all.

I am delighted to hear that Edith has been able to stay on at the school, and I hope that will continue. But I'm extremely worried about Wolfgang. My enquiries after his address have remained unanswered and I haven't heard a word from him since July, so you can imagine how anxious I am. Are you still practising hard at the violin? It would be so lovely if we could all get together again, and you could demonstrate your new talents! You know how much we enjoy listening to music. Often I picture in my mind what it will be like when we finally see each other again! But when will that be, and where?!

Can you still remember your birthday two years ago? – I gave you chocolates and the two of us sat on the sofa at lunchtime, tucking in! It was just lovely, and we have so many wonderful memories like this to be thankful for! And soon it will be our little Edith's birthday! I wonder whether I'll get post that day too! I long for it.

Papa will write again in a few days' time and we hope that at least one of our letters will get to you.

> I send all three of you
> countless sweet and loving kisses,
> Mama
> Warmest kisses, dear child, from your Papa

26 March 1941
Düsseldorf

PARENTS TO EVA-MARIA

My dear child,

You simply can't imagine how thrilled we were to get your letter of 19 November right on your birthday, and what's more it gave us answers to questions we'd asked in a letter we sent you on the day of our silver wedding anniversary! Mama had always predicted that we'd get news from you on that day. I tried to talk her out of it to prevent disappointment, but she refused to be put off and the mother's heart was proved right.

Mama and I are both in very good health. Everything is fine here, and just as it was when you were all here. Grandma is well too. We've just received a note from her – she was delighted to read your letter, and asks us to send you her regards. Uncle Josi and Aunt Bertha are also well and on very good form; they've just had their first letter from Peter, which we've read, and he seems fine.

Since your letter was written only a week after your previous one of 11 November, your circumstances had not changed in the interim. We hope that you've since been released from the internment camp. We asked the Red Cross to try to obtain information about all three of you, and were informed that Fräulein Fritz, the Perrys and the Cottons had all offered to take you in when you are released. I hope you've made the right choice there. The Red Cross were also able to tell us that Edith is now Deputy Headmistress at the Ancaster School in Penn. Is that correct, or have we misunderstood? Is she in fact Deputy Matron?* We have heard nothing about Wolfgang. All we hear from you and the Red Cross is that he is interned, and that he's well, but nobody has given us his address even though we've asked for it repeatedly. I'm sure you can understand how worried we are. Still, it's a good thing that the three of you are able to communicate with one another.

Our life goes on as it always has, and I am still working. Work is progressing well and doesn't appear to have declined at all. – We celebrate Grandma's 83rd birthday on 3 April. She might come and see us for a few days, and if not I'll go and visit her.

There's a letter from us on its way to Edith. We wish for nothing more than to have good news from you all as soon as possible, and to hear something from Wolfgang finally. We hope from the bottom of our hearts that you are all well

---

* Edith was not interned, and since 1939 she had been working as a teacher in various schools; it is therefore more likely that she was Deputy Headmistress at the school.

and lack for nothing, and that you're coping well in these difficult times.

Warmest kisses, my dear child, from your Papa

Today you're only going to get a short note from me, my dear girl, as with any luck you'll have had my letter only a few days ago! I just wish we would hear some conclusive news of Wolfgang! That's what worries us most – at least we have some sign of life from you two occasionally. Be brave, and have faith in God's help!

Warmest, sweetest kisses to the three of you,
from Mama

Easter Monday 1941
Düsseldorf

PARENTS TO EVA-MARIA
My beloved child,

Your sweet letter of 3 January arrived just in time for Easter, and we couldn't have had a better Easter present. We are always so happy even just to see your handwriting again – this allows us to believe that you are in good health, and that we can still hope to have a happy reunion some day, when all this suffering has come to an end. One week ago – on Grandma's 83rd birthday, in fact – we finally received some long-awaited news from Wolfgang, and he is apparently well. It was only a communication from the Red Cross, so nothing more personal, but we were delighted and grateful that they enclosed the original letter he sent to them, asking them to inform us that he is in Australia! There's no date given. The poor boy is still so young, and yet he's been shunted off to the other side of the world. We can only hope that he remains honest and good, and that he doesn't come under the influence of any bad elements while he's abroad. Can you write to him regularly? I always thought that he would write us a letter, as all internees are allowed to, but sadly we've not had anything yet.

You don't even mention in your letter what you're doing. We very much hope that things are going as well for you as they were in November, and that you're still together with the same people you were so fond of at the time. It's wonderful news that Edith had such a fine Christmas, and even better that she's doing a job that she likes and can really excel in. In two weeks it's her birthday, and I wonder whether post will arrive here on that day, as it did on yours!

I'm to pass on best wishes from all our relatives and friends, and from the Pastor and his wife etc., etc. Ruth wants me to tell you that she went to a class reunion recently, and everybody there asked after you and sends their regards, especially your last class teacher. And Ruth of course sends extra special greetings.

On Friday I went to Communion, and Papa and I went to church again yesterday. When I'm there I can picture you standing next to me, and despite our separation I feel so close to you all. I live in constant hope of seeing you all again, and that's the only thing that keeps me going. But please, I don't want any of you to worry about us. Our life is still entirely unchanged; we're living on our own in peace and quiet and, thank the Lord, we're both very well. We are

quite satisfied if we get a positive letter from one of you once
in a while, and we continue to hope for a better future.
Please look after your health, you three, and make sure that
whatever happens you keep your faith in God – as long as
you do, everything will turn out fine! I embrace all three of
you, and give each of you a big kiss!

Your Mama

PS Many warm kisses, my dear child, from your Papa. I'll
write again very soon.

19 April 1941
Düsseldorf

PARENTS TO EVA-MARIA
Dear child,

Your internee's letter of 3 January has arrived, and
yesterday we also got your Red Cross message of 2 January.
Mama has already answered the letter, and I'm writing
again, as before, just in case her letter doesn't get to you.

We are quite reassured with everything you've written.
You say that both you and Edith are well, and yet we haven't
heard a thing from Edith for months. We hope that you will
be released soon, and that you will make the right decision
about where to stay afterwards. It's quite marvellous that
Edith was able to have such lovely Christmas holidays.

For quite some time we'd actually been wondering
whether Wolfgang had been interned in a completely different part of the world. Quite understandably our main
concern was whether or not he'd arrived there safe and
sound. And then just as we'd got back from visiting Grand-

ma for her birthday we got the letter from the Red Cross in Geneva informing us of Wolfgang's internment in Australia, and giving his address. Your long letter arrived two weeks after your birthday, and that told us more. We are of course very sad that he is now so far away from us all, but we share your opinion that for the moment it's probably for the best, and that he'll be much safer there.

We are happy and proud that the three of you are making such a success of your lives abroad, even if the thoughts that sustain you are of your home here. This makes us realise that we have fulfilled our duties with you all, and considering all our current hardships that's not always been easy. If you've been able to make the right choices when you've had to do so on your own, it will be all the better when the five of us can be together once again. I find it quite wonderful how the three of you stick together; it was sweet of Edith to send a Christmas parcel to Wolfgang, even though I am sure she has very little money to spare, and of you to send him a telegram for Christmas and his birthday. All this fills us with great confidence for your future, and for ours too.

Everything is fine here, and quite unchanged. I continue to work as much as I can, and my writing is progressing well. Grandma is on good form, as are Aunt Bertha and Uncle Josef. We always send the three of them copies of your letters, which they are as pleased to receive as we are, and they all send you much love.

My little girl, you and the others must keep your spirits up, and please be brave until all this is over!

                    Loving kisses to you all, from Papa

My good child, I've decided to add a little greeting to this after all, but I hope you've also got the letter I wrote on Easter Monday. I wonder when we'll get your next one?! Here the weather is beautiful and springlike, and I so wish I could be enjoying it with you again!

> I send infinite kisses and a very big hug
> to all three of you, your Mama

24 April 1941
Düsseldorf

PARENTS TO WOLFGANG

My beloved boy,

When your dear letter arrived here after such a dreadfully long silence, it was the best day we'd had in a very, very long time. Two weeks ago the Geneva Red Cross informed us that you are in Australia, and they sent us the original letter you'd sent to them. In the meantime we've also had a letter from Eva-Maria saying that she and Edith had both heard from you, and that you're fine. Edith also sent us a note via the Red Cross, and so even if I only hear from you all occasionally, I must be satisfied that you are well.

How are you passing the time over there? I hope it's possible for you to learn something that might be useful later in your professional life. You are still so young, with your whole life ahead of you. If only I could be sure that you are behaving, and that you're not forgetting everything we've tried to impress upon you: remember to tackle everything as energetically as you can, and to be loyal and honourable always!

Is it possible for you to go to church over there? Please

make sure you keep your faith in God, and remember that one day all this will be over!

Grandma, Aunt Bertha, Uncle Josef, and your friend Herbert, his brother and parents are all fine, and they send you their very best regards.

I do so hope to have another letter from you soon, but for today much love, my dear child, and an awfully big hug

from Mama

My dear, dear boy,

We are so happy to have news of you at last! We have been terribly worried about our Wolfgang. I'm typing this letter as my heavy handwriting will show through the paper otherwise. In the next few days I'll write you another letter in case this one doesn't arrive. Be brave and look after yourself! Everything will turn out fine. We heard from Eva-Maria that your former departmental boss wrote you a very good reference. Try to be good at the camp too and do us credit!

Loving kisses,

Papa

20 May 1941
Düsseldorf

PARENTS TO EVA-MARIA

My beloved daughter,

We were so happy to get your letter, but at the same time rather depressed as you write that none of you have heard from us since September. We're convinced, however, that at least one of the many letters we've sent to the three of you must have arrived in the meantime. Even Grandma has written to both you and Wolfgang.

Everything's just fine here, and really nothing has changed. I am still spending my time on the same projects; my work gives me a great deal of pleasure, and it's going quite well. We're assuming that you've been released by now and have made your way to the Cottons, this being the best option for you.

We're glad to know that Edith is so happy with her job, and I'm assuming she must be employed at a Rudolf Steiner school. We also received the Red Cross message you sent together in December, and we were delighted with it. I can of course understand that your separation from the friends you made in the camp has made you quite despondent, but you can be sure that you will see them all again. Friendships like that often last for life. I am delighted that you're still learning the violin. I wonder whether there will soon come a time when you'll be able to play us something. How did you get on with your history talks? Well, my dear child, stay well, be good, keep your courage and hold fast to the hope that one day everything will improve and we will see each other again.

With many many loving kisses to the three of you,

Papa

My dear good girl,

Now you've been away for more than two years, and the others for more than four! We've managed to survive this long time quite well, and we must live in the hope that it won't be as long before we see each other again. We've only had one letter from Wolfgang so far, even though others who are there seem to write more often! I hope he and you two are all well. I imagine I might get post from you again any day now and I hope I won't be disappointed?! Ten days ago we sent another note to Edith via the Red Cross.

A very big hug and kisses from your Mama

The Lindemeyer parents' response to Eva-Maria's Red Cross communication of 28 May 1941, reproduced on the adjacent page

6 *August 1941*
Düsseldorf

Happy about news! Why not give your address? Where's Wolfgang to go after release? Terribly long time without his news. Glad about your jobs!

Loving kisses, Mama, Papa

8 *November 1941*
Düsseldorf

FRIEDA TO EDITH, EVA-MARIA AND WOLFGANG
My dearest three,

A year has passed since I wrote the enclosed letter. When I wrote it last November, we feared that we might be driven out like those people in Baden.* After that I thought I wouldn't be able to go on, and I considered putting an end

---

* In October 1940 approximately 6,500 Jews were deported from the Baden and Saarpfalz areas.

*Eva-Maria's Red Cross communication
to her parents of 28 May 1941*

to this unbearable torment. Since then a year has passed, a year so full of grief and suffering, but we have always managed to keep a roof over our heads.

But now everything has changed. Tomorrow, in the cruellest circumstances, we are being forced to leave our house, and will be deported to another country. Our destination is probably Minsk. Now we have to abandon everything that we held dear and go abroad without a pfennig in our pockets. This is no minor matter for people of our age. After an extremely difficult inner struggle I have decided not to leave Papa alone, although if I knew that I'd never be able to see you all again I would prefer to go to sleep for ever. I will try to hold out, and I'll pray to God to give me the strength to bear all these dreadful things that He brings upon us. I do not know for how long or whether I will be able to do this. I am a sick person, and yet they are still driving me out! May God grant that we see one another again, despite everything! I pray to God every day and every hour that He may preserve and protect me, and that the time will come when we will be reunited! If it should turn out differently, at least you will know how much I have hoped and prayed for you. Should we be destined not to see each other again, then you must bear it nobly – never forget that life had become unbearable for us, and let us rest in peace! Our first and last thought will always be of you three, my beloved children! Now we have spent our last night in our own bed, beneath our own protective roof. Now we are to be sent away, yet still we hope it is with God at our side! Pray for us, just as we send our prayers up to heaven only for you. Become people we would have been proud to call our children. Do not forget all those things we experienced together! If Ilse Peters should still live, you must honour her always – she was the best friend I could have wished for. May the Lord God bless and protect you all!

The following letter was written by Frieda Lindemeyer on 1 November 1940.

My dearly beloved children!

I am forced to write these words to you as we do not know whether we will be granted a reunion with you on this earth. Every hour there is the possibility that a bomb will put an end to our lives, but it is equally possible that other causes will bring about our premature death. If you should at some point learn that I have died in such a way that makes you wonder how I could possibly have done this to you, my children, then I beg you all to try to understand, and please believe that I had no choice. I think I know you too well to imagine that you would demand the impossible of me. I know that you love me too much for that. I am writing these lines without knowing if they will ever reach you, nor do I know whether there has been any point to all my waiting and suffering, and whether you three are still there! How dreadfully we all have to suffer, without even knowing what we have done to deserve such a fate. For me the worst thing will always be my separation from you, my beloved children, and the uncertainty over your futures. I would find all this easier to bear if only I knew that you were all well, with a roof over your heads and food on your plates, and that you were together with good people. I am sure that you long for us, just as we long for you. We must bow to our fate and hope that the day will come when I will be able to collect this letter from the bank myself and hold the three of you in my arms again.

But if the Lord our God decides otherwise for us, then I must say to you Farewell! To you first of all, my dearest eldest! You will always have to be the big sister to the other two, setting them a good example in life. And you, my little Edith! Keep up the energy with which you have tackled life at such a young age. With these qualities you can be a great help and support to one another. How often I think of that time you telephoned when war was threatened, and you begged us to let you come home. I do not have the words to express how difficult it has been for me to leave you there, especially with the prospect of what now unavoidably awaits us. And yet I had to stand firm; I could not weaken. Life here would have become completely impossible for you all. So I had to act as I did, despite what I most longed and wished for. And now to you, my dear, good boy! I hope that you retain your willingness to help others, and that gaiety which will help you through difficult times! I wish for all of you that life will repay you the love that you have shown me during these difficult years. I thank you, my beloved children, for each hour of your lives – you were my whole happiness and my joy.

My most fervent wish is that each of you finds the companion destined for you in life, with whom you can build the home that life has prematurely deprived you of. I would need countless hours to tell you all the things I have to say but – since this is the way it has to be – instead I say to you farewell, and with the most profound feelings of love I hold all three of you close to my heart,

                                    your Mama

My greatest plea is that you remember to pray, and do not forget the Lord our God.

                                    9 November 1941
                                    Düsseldorf

GEORG TO EVA-MARIA, EDITH AND WOLFGANG
Beloved children,

I wrote the enclosed letter one year ago. What I feared already then has today come to pass: we and our fellow sufferers are being forced to leave Düsseldorf, and we're to be deported to the East, apparently to Minsk. We have tried to inform Eva-Maria of this in a note sent via the Red Cross.

Today I have nothing to add to what I have said in the enclosed letter. We put our entire trust in God and hope that He will lead us by the hand as He has until now, and that He will bring the five of us together again.

                    With warmest kisses from your father

The following letter was written by Georg Lindemeyer on 1 November 1940.

My beloved children,

We have talked about you every day, and thought of you

constantly. I was convinced that we would see one another again, and I am still convinced today. I have written these lines in case things should turn out differently.

We have had no direct news from you for a long time, and we are concerned that you are still alive and well. Pray God that you are. If we do not see one another again, please do not change from how we have known you as children. Should you be faced with a difficult and consequential decision, then just imagine that the five of us are sitting round our dining-room table, and you are telling us all what you would like to do. Your instincts will say to you whether or not we would agree. We have drawn up our will in accordance with the current legal requirements in Germany. We believe that by doing so we have provided for everything in the best way possible. Once again, as I mention in my will, I make it your solemn duty to see to it that my manuscripts are published – otherwise my life's work has been in vain. This is the best manifestation of my trust in you all. We have always done everything for you that has been in our power.

So, my beloved children, be happy.

A kiss from your father

OUR LAST WILL AND TESTAMENT

If we should die at the same time, or if one of us should die so soon after the other that the surviving partner is unable to draw up a Last Will and Testament, then our sole heir is to be my sister, Frau Bertha Sara Meyer, of Elberfelder-strasse 7, Berlin NW87. As soon as it becomes possible again, my sister is to support our children with all available means, as far as this is permissible, and also call in the full extent of our capital. In addition, she is to pay a monthly maintenance contribution to my mother-in-law, Frau Mathilde Sara Hobbie, of 28 Kirschbaumstrasse, Wuppertal-Elberfeld, until her death, the amount of which is to be decided by my sister in accordance with reasonable estimation, and which is to correspond to circumstances in general and to my sister's financial situation.

Frau Frieda Sara Lindemeyer, née Lewinsky
Düsseldorf, 19 February 1940

The above will of my wife may also be regarded as my own in the event that our deaths should happen in this way. My most important manuscripts can be found in deposit box number 11977 at the Deutsche Bank in Düsseldorf, and the rest are in my writing desk. It is my wish that my children do their utmost to have them published in succession. I ask our heir, my sister-in-law, to communicate this wish to my children when this will comes into force and as soon as it is possible for her to do so. My sister-in-law is to arrange for their publication only with the agreement of my children. I hereby request that my sister-in-law removes the manuscripts from the deposit box and from the drawer of my desk, and stores them in a deposit box at a bank in Berlin. A copy of this will can be found in deposit box number 11977. The key to this and a ticket to gain admission to the vault can both be found in the money box in the top drawer of my writing desk.

Dr Georg Israel Lindemeyer
Düsseldorf, 19 February 1940

14 *November 1941*
Berlin

AUNT BERTHA TO EVA-MARIA
 [communication via the Red Cross]
Your September news arrived unexpected. Parents left Düsseldorf. Will send address ASAP. Send letters here. Reunion expected. Stay brave, healthy, trust in God. Warmest kisses, Bertha, Josi.

The Lindemeyer children never heard from their parents again. The letters that follow here are the responses of friends, relations and officials to their efforts to discover more about their parents' fate.

12 March 1943
London

RED CROSS TO EVA-MARIA
Dear Madam,

We have received your letter of 10 March, and are very sorry that we cannot give you any news of your parents' welfare or whereabouts.

We have written to the International Red Cross Committee at Geneva again today and asked them to do all in their power to get news of your parents for you. We shall write to you as soon as we get a reply from Geneva. But we fear that it may take six to eight months as these enquiries are becoming increasingly difficult to make. We are afraid there is no possibility at the moment for people in enemy-occupied countries to come to this country. The enemy does not allow them to leave the country.

Yours truly,
P. Layward
p.p. M. M. Carden
C. M. Section

10 April 1945
London

RED CROSS TO EVA-MARIA
Dear Madam,

Thank you for your letter of 30 March. We greatly fear that it may still take some time before any steps can be taken to obtain news of people deported to Poland, as the Russian authorities have asked me to defer all such investigations until the military situation is more settled.

We understand and sympathise very deeply with you in your anxiety, but we can assure you that we will communicate with you as soon as we receive any news about your parents, or any information about what has happened to the people who were interned at Minsk. We are so sorry not to be able to help you more at the moment, but do hope we may soon be able to obtain some reassuring news.

Yours truly,
[signature illegible]

2 February 1946
Düsseldorf

ILSE PETERS TO HERR ROSEN

Dear Herr Rosen,

It is with great sorrow that I have to inform you that I have found no further trace of Frieda and Georg since they were forced to leave Düsseldorf on 27 October 1941,* and I can no longer believe that they are alive. I have just begun to track down the addresses of people who left Düsseldorf on the same transport to Minsk and have now returned. As soon as I have made contact with them, I will write to you again.

---

* This was the date of the first transport from Düsseldorf, to Lodz. In fact the Lindemeyers were deported to Minsk on 10 November 1941.

Georg's manuscripts are in my safe. There are also a few items of their belongings here in my house: a bookcase; a metal preserving pan and a box of mementoes. Herr Hamacher took most of the furniture with him to Berlin when he moved there with his family. It is being stored with Hermann Knorr, who owns a garage at 19 Prinz Heinrichstrasse, Berlin-Karlshorst (the train station is Berlin-Rummelsburg). I have not yet established whether the furniture has survived the war. As I have now written extensively to Berlin, I am now passing this information on to you so that you can get in touch with them yourself.

Yours,
Ilse Peters

10 April 1946
Düsseldorf

ILSE PETERS TO EVA-MARIA
Dear Eva-Maria,

We are so happy to be back in touch with the three of you, and to know that you are well! Many thanks for your letter and for the two photographs, which I look at often. If only I had better news for you! This is a difficult letter for me to write. During the worst period of bombing I often said: 'None of this is as bad as the day the Lindemeyers were deported.'

I have a friend who works at the Deutsche Bank in Königsallee, and he was able to establish that the deposit box has long since been transferred to someone else. He's going to find out when this happened, and who returned the key. I can scarcely believe that your father would have maintained the deposit box: first of all because he would surely have mentioned it to me, and secondly because he must have reckoned that its contents would be confiscated. This is why I think those manuscripts he gave me right at the end (which Wolfgang has now brought over to you) are the ones he kept in the box. It's also possible that this is where he kept the will, and he forgot to change what he'd written in it about the deposit box. Or was their will only written in the days just before their deportation?

You ask why your parents didn't flee the country. Well, rather cunningly this had been made all but impossible: from spring 1941* all Jews were forced to wear the Star of David. It's something that should have been a sign of honour, but in fact it was a dreadful act of cruelty. If anyone so much as spoke to a Jew they could count on being reported and severely punished.

The Star of David also made it very difficult for someone to hide. After it was imposed, your poor mother hardly left home. In addition, Jews were forbidden to travel without special permission. In the last weeks this was particularly hard for your father as his mother was ill, and he was extremely demoralised by the complicated process he had to undergo to obtain permission to go and see her in Elberfeld. Your father tried repeatedly to be exempted from this by getting a doctor's certificate for your mother. She was never particularly unwell, but all the upset caused her the most

---

* The compulsory wearing of the Star of David for Jews was introduced only in September 1941, not in spring of that year, as is suggested here.

terrible cramps. It was simply too awful that no one would take that into account. But your father's hope that an exemption might have a decisive influence was not fulfilled either. After that he was counting on the imminent collapse of the regime, and yet this still took another two and a half years. The priest who gave us Communion was in fact Pastor Balke, who now lives in Neviges (in the Rhineland). He was Pastor Hötzel's successor in caring for Christian non-Aryans, and he was loyal and courageous in his work. Pastor Homann came by afterwards, in fact he visited your mother several times in those final days. He strengthened her resolve not to take her own life, although the temptation for her to do so was great. But in the end even your father said quite clearly and firmly: 'No, that is something one must not do. Our lives are in God's hands!' But I would have found all this simply unbearable had I not witnessed with each of your parents how trust in God can bring peace to the heart – even in the worst circumstances. I must finish for now. I will come and see you as soon as I can to tell you everything that I know.

Very best wishes from Ilse Peters

26 April 1946
Düsseldorf

ILSE PETERS TO EDITH
Dear Edith,

I think I may already have answered your main question in my last letter. The temptation for them to end their lives in those days leading up to their expulsion was of course tremendous, particularly for your father, who deeply dreaded being deprived of all possibility to continue with his intellectual endeavours. There was not much I could say to them on the subject – after all, I was being allowed to stay. I just tried to reiterate to them both that there can be no state of wretchedness into which God's hand does not pass. And Pastor Homann stood firm and told them: 'You cannot do it.' I agreed with him.

I do not know whether your parents regretted not having gone through with it. When they left they had no idea of how difficult things would become. Above all they believed that they would still be able to receive post, and for them the fact that this was made impossible was probably the worst thing of all. But despite such bitter disappointments, I do believe that it was this very solitude which kept them at one with God, and they learned that if they were to end their lives for fear of what they might have to suffer, they would forgo God's blessing.

I'm sure I have already told you that I stayed in their apartment that last night and slept on the chaise longue in the sitting room. I must admit that I kept listening out for them fearfully. Oh, I would have understood it, of course. But they struggled on through that night too, and I think they even managed to sleep for a while.

With all best wishes to you and Eva-Maria

Yours,

Ilse Peters

28 April 1946
Düsseldorf

HILDEGARD WEGNER TO EVA-MARIA

My dear Eva-Maria,

We were so glad to hear from you all at last, after all these years, and to hold your dear letter in our hands. Thank you so much for it, and for the charming photographs. None of you have changed a bit, and I still remember your green woollen dress with the silver chain!

It's rather a shame that Wolfgang isn't stationed in Düsseldorf. It was such a surprise to see him standing there on the doorstep, so big and tall, and grinning at me. 'It's me, Wolfgang!' he said, and I was so terribly happy I cried: 'At last!' Now he's a fully grown man. I was glad that he was able to tell me himself about your lives over there, and it makes me happy to think that you three are together in your own sweet little home. I cannot tell you how hard it is for me to write about your parents, because no words can express what my heart wants to say. I have always dreaded this moment, and wondered how I would tell you about the most difficult thing you could possibly have to deal with. How must you have felt all this time, not knowing anything for certain, but always hearing the most terrible reports? We knew the dreadful truth much sooner, as sometimes we had reports from soldiers. I have been thinking of you constantly, and I have prayed that you would be strong enough to bear the awful certainty.

Unfortunately I don't know any details about conditions in Minsk, nor have I been able to make contact with anyone who has returned from there. Before their deportation I was often together with your dear parents, even during the final days, and I constantly implored them to flee. Of course there was scarcely any possibility for them to escape, but my opinion is and has always been: where there's a will, there's a way. Your parents didn't consider my suggestions that they go to Switzerland, and your mother, normally so active, was extremely tired and despondent, and believed that she would have to give in to her fate. But I have to emphasise once again that the chances of somebody being able to remain in hiding were very slim indeed.

I am so dreadfully sorry for you all that your father's manuscripts have been destroyed. He entrusted them to me as his most precious legacy to you. The family photographs I was to look after for you have also been destroyed, as all these things were kept in that part of the cellar that was burnt out. The other part was saved, thanks to the intervention of a soldier, and there we mainly kept the furniture we were storing for relatives from Cologne who had been deported to Lodz. There are also a few of your father's books (mainly classics and philosophy) and a small plaque that he must have been awarded for something.

As far as the radio is concerned, I seem to remember that it was confiscated by the Gestapo some time before your parents even left Düsseldorf, and the same goes for the telephone. Unfortunately I know nothing more about what happened with the house in Göttingen. I do remember that your parents either had to take out a mortgage because of the expropriation laws, or they sold it. At the time we spoke about it a great deal.

Dearest Eva-Maria, should I not have told you all this? It will all weigh terribly upon you. But I think I can say from my own experience that even these awful truths can be better for the soul's resilience than a constant uncertainty, which could completely wear you down. Please be brave – your beloved parents are now in peace. Had they returned they would almost certainly have been broken people, and they wouldn't have been able to enjoy life any longer.

I send you a thousand warm wishes and a loving kiss,

your old Hilde

5 May 1946
Meerbusch

DR WERNER KARTHAUS TO EVA-MARIA, EDITH
AND WOLFGANG

Dear Eva-Maria, Edith and Wolfgang,

We have often talked of the three of you and your parents, and we remember very well all the times we spent together. With you we deeply mourn the tragic fate of your dear parents – it is a terrible thing, that all hope of finding them is now gone, and their beloved children will feel this more than anyone else. But you can be certain that Aunt Hilde and I genuinely share in your painful emotions!

Indeed, I do remember several of your father's works; we still own his book 'Aryan and Semitic Literature', and if you'd like it we'd very gladly send it to you. We enjoyed a particularly close intellectual exchange at the time he was working on his tragic play, 'Savonarola', and also writing critical essays on literature. – I don't know much more about the drama, nor can I give you any more detail on the essays I've just mentioned. But I still have a very vivid and precise picture of what he wanted to do with the essays that he was going to put together in a book. Each essay contained a precise technical and psychological analysis of a major play in world literature. I remember 'Berenice', 'Wallenstein' and others very well. Taken together, these essays were to represent a history of dramatic works in the literature of the world seen from an artistic point of view. Your father wanted to prove how the influence of Greek drama in world literature was still very much alive.

But for him this thesis wasn't the most important thing, nor was a dry anatomy of the plays; instead, in this highly significant work, he was able to give wonderfully vivid insights into the rules of drama, and managed to appreciate the peculiarities of each writer with such acute reasoning and affectionate understanding. The reader could not fail to recognise two things: a rather rare knowledge of his subject and a great love of art, which were matched by a dramatic talent of his own – only a real expert can analyse and understand the works of others with such brilliance!

The dominant image of your father that comes to mind is one of a great idealist whose interests were in fact purely intellectual, and who in his artistic endeavours could not easily find his match. For me at any rate my association with him, and our exchange of ideas, was extremely valuable, and I will remember the inspiration he has given me with gratitude!

> With our best wishes to you all, and greetings
> from Uncle Werner and Aunt Hilde

7 June 1946
Kronach

REINHARD HOBBIE TO EVA-MARIA, EDITH AND WOLFGANG
Dear Eva-Maria, Edith and Wolfgang,

You can imagine how delighted we were to hear that the three of you are well – we thought it likely that you were, but we couldn't be absolutely sure.

I'm afraid I don't know very much about your parents' fate, but the little I do know I will gladly share with you: in the middle of November 1941, your father sent a goodbye letter to us in Bautzen (where we were once again living), in which he told us that he and your mother were to be sent to the East together with about one hundred others who shared their fate. Of course the tone of the letter was subdued, but not completely despairing, and I'm certain your parents didn't know what awaited them – nor did we at the time. For example, his letter spoke of an 'imminent reunion'. We took that to mean that your parents hoped for a swift end to the war and liberation by foreign troops, and at the time we thought no differently, for nobody could have imagined that thoroughly corrupt system could have kept going for such a long time. The only news I had received of them after this letter was a message from a pastor in Wuppertal saying that the transport had arrived in Minsk, although this could not be established with absolute certainty.

I know very little about your father's manuscripts: I was aware that he devoted much of his time to writing about aspects of literary history and literary theory, and also legal theory. This work certainly meant a great deal to him, and probably helped him through difficult times. Several of his essays were published in a Swiss literary journal, but unfortunately I have forgotten its name.

I'm afraid I know nothing at all, however, about the sale of the house, nor do I have details of any securities. I am so sorry not to be able to help, but I was not given any instructions on those matters, and you have to remember that the considerable distance between Düsseldorf and Bautzen probably meant that things happened there that I would have heard nothing about.

Your grandmother died around the time that your parents were deported. She had been ill for a long time, and at the end she was so weak that she was no longer aware of much that was going on around her, so your parents' fate could be kept from her. She really only suffered at the very end (with dropsy). In her will she left an oil painting for your parents and you three, a landscape of Lake Starnberg painted after the Impressionists. It's rather valuable, as I discovered when an art dealer made me an offer for it. There is also a man's pocket watch in gold with a spring lid, and several silver spoons. The painting is well packed and is being stored with a forwarding agent in Elberfeld; Aunt Gertrud was there a short time ago and was satisfied that it was being well looked after. Aunt Gertrud sends her warmest wishes, which I heartily endorse!

Yours,
Uncle Reinhard

14 September 1946
Düsseldorf-Oberkassel

ILSE PETERS TO EDITH AND EVA-MARIA

Dear Edith and Eva-Maria,

A long time has passed since I received your joint letter of 3 July, for which many thanks. You write so animatedly that it's almost as if you were both here beside me, but I still so look forward to the moment when we do finally see one another again. Sadly I think it might be some time yet before that will be possible.

You still have so many questions for me, and there's so much you want to know. Your greatest concern is whether they had to endure life in Minsk for long. I don't think so. They arrived there in November 1941. The two men I spoke to who had also been in Minsk do not remember that they survived beyond August 1942. They did not see them after that, so that's eight months, and those first months would have been the most bearable. People still had the clothes they'd brought with them, which they could exchange for food using the Russians as intermediaries. They were given small houses in a designated neighbourhood in Minsk, and they would have been able to furnish them reasonably well. They would have found various household articles and kitchen implements there, and I think everyone had what they basically needed. I couldn't get very much information out of those who returned.

If I think back to the time when your parents were still here, I can always remember how many people took pains to show them that they wanted nothing to do with official anti-Semitism. For example, the people who ran the grocery your mother went to always treated her particularly well. At the time you could occasionally still get oranges on your ration card, and more than once your mother gave me some. With her card she wasn't supposed to get any at all, but the grocer secretly stuffed many more into her bag than anyone else ever got. I also know that the overseer responsible for your father at the cemetery kept saying how terrible he felt that your father was forced to do that kind of work, and he always tried to make things as easy as possible: he allowed plenty of time for breaks and gave the weaker men lighter work, etc.

So, no, 'the German people' was not anti-Semitic. And when they began with these dreadful deportations, more than once I saw both simple and educated people on the street strike up a conversation and say to each other: 'This cannot and will not end well. This will be avenged upon us.' The bomb attack that destroyed our apartments was felt by many to be punishment for the fact that Jewish homes had been ransacked in November 1938.

With very best wishes to both of you, from my father and sisters too.

Yours,
Ilse Peters

3 December 1946
Burg

THE HAMACHER FAMILY TO EVA-MARIA, EDITH
   AND WOLFGANG

My dearest three,

So the siblings are finally back together again. We properly celebrated Wolfgang's visit here – we were so delighted to see him. It sounds as though you are all very happy in your dear little home; I thank you in particular, my dear Eva-Maria, for writing us such a sweet letter about your lives over there.

Yes, my Eva-Maria, what I set down in my letter were more or less the last conversations I had with your mother. She was lying on the chaise longue in the dining room, trying to gather her strength for the trip to the assembly point. My husband and Fräulein Peters were packing up the last items your parents were allowed to bring with them, such as down quilts and duvets. Your father was in the smoking room and I sat holding hands with your mother, as I did so often in those last few days.

In those last hours I spent with your mother – during which we barely spoke, but instead allowed our souls to communicate with each other – we never once talked of our parting. Your Mama often closed her eyes, and I stroked her and surrounded her with all my love to help her through those difficult hours. Then we embraced and gave each other a sisterly kiss, and I left quietly. I felt then that I no longer had the strength to remain calm and composed, and Mama was also trying her utmost to keep herself together.

My husband had left in the meantime, and I crept out without saying goodbye to Fräulein Peters – I simply couldn't. In the stairwell I could finally allow my tears to flow. We had agreed that I would leave half an hour before them – your mother would be stronger if we were not there.

Eva-Maria, Edith, in my thoughts I embrace you. This has been a difficult letter to write, but you should know, in fact you wanted to know, how it was!

Warmest wishes for Christmas,
from the Hamacher family

27 January 1947
Düsseldorf

ILSE PETERS TO EVA-MARIA AND EDITH
Dear Eva-Maria and Edith,

Your things are of course still safely stored with us here. You'll just have to let us know in advance when they'll be collected, as they're all stacked in different places. Also, I'm afraid I have to tell you that I cut your father's name out of all his books. We always had to be prepared for a house search, and it would have been too dangerous. I hope you will understand.

It appears as though they are slowly beginning the hearings for damages payments to parties who have been injured as a result of the National-Socialist regime. I'm sure you'll have heard about it, and it seems that you have somebody who will be representing your affairs. I hope something good comes of it. We wish you all the best for the New Year, even though we're nearly at the end of its first month.

With best regards from my sister and myself,
Ilse Peters

Wolfgang

Edith

Eva-Maria

The Lindemeyer children in the early 1940s

2031 Club Boulevard, Durham, N.C. U.S.A. April 12.

Sehr geehrter Herr Lindemeyer, mit gleicher Post sende ich Ihnen eingeschrieben 6 verschiedene Papiere ein, die Affidavits für Sie und Ihre Frau und die sonst erforderlichen Auskunftspapiere über den Affidavitspender. Der Sicherheit halber schicke ich noch diese Karte, und bitte Sie, mir den Empfang der Papiere umgehend zu melden. Hoffentlich dauert es nicht zu lange, bis die Yorkstr. sich in eine in N.Y. umwandelt! Ich wünsche Ihnen bestes Gelingen und hoffe, wenn auch das Herkommen sich verzögern dürfte nach allem, was man über die Nummern hört, so doch, dass Sie irgendwo im Grünen die Zeit abwarten können. Es wird mich freuen, bald Günstiges von der Entwicklung Ihrer Bemühungen zu hören.

Mit freundlichen Grüssen Ihre
Urs. William Stern.

2031 Club Boulevard, Durham, N.C. USA
12 April 1939

Dear Herr Lindemeyer,

I am sending by registered post 6 separate documents: affidavits for you and your wife together with forms giving the information required about the provider of the affidavit. In order to be absolutely safe, I am sending you this postcard as well, so please let me know when you receive the documents. Hopefully it won't be too long before you can exchange York Street for one in New York! I wish you every success and hope that even if their arrival is delayed (which seems to happen all the time at the moment) you can spend the intervening period in the fresh air somewhere. I look forward to hearing soon of a positive outcome to your efforts.

With best wishes,
Yours,
William Stern

Found among Georg and Frieda's papers was this letter which
promised them asylum in America.

Dramatis Personae

(in alphabetical order)

ANDREAS SALOMÉ, Lou: a German writer and a friend of Frieda's uncle Alfred Cöhn. She also knew the poet Rainer Maria Rilke, and a correspondence between them was published in 1952.

AUNT BERTHA: see MEYER, Bertha and Josef.

AUNT GERTRUD: see HOBBIE, Dr Reinhard and Gertrud.

AUNT HANNI: see PHILIPPSOHN, Hanni and Leo.

AUNT ILSE: see LEWINSKY, Paul and Ilse.

AUNT MARTHA: see CÖHN, Dr Alfred and Martha.

AUNT MATHILDE: see CÖHN, Richard and Mathilde.

AUNT TILLY: see Peartree, Tilly.

BARMÉ, Margarete: one of the coordinators of the Wuppertal branch of the Paulusbund.

BARSHALL, Miss: employee of the Inter-Aid Committee, with particular responsibility for the 'aftercare' of refugee children once they had arrived in England.

BERGENTHAL, Dr Max: Düsseldorf GP who fled to England with his wife after their flat was destroyed during the night of the pogrom in November 1938.

BÖLLERT, Erna, Hanna and Leoni (referred to as Lony): friends of the Lindemeyers whom they met through the network of Christians of Jewish origin in Düsseldorf. Their mother, Ernestine, was deported to Theresienstadt in July 1942.

BOLTON, Mr: headmaster of Magdalen College School, Brackley, which Wolfgang attended on his arrival in England.

CASALTA, Martha: Frieda Lindemeyer's closest school-friend.

CASSWELL, Mr and Mrs: friends of the Perry family, with whom Eva-Maria lived in London.

CÖHN, Dr Alfred and Martha: Frieda Lindemeyer's uncle and his wife. He was Professor of Chemistry at Göttingen University until 1929. Eva-Maria lived with him from September 1937 until his death in March 1938. Frieda was the sole inheritor of his estate.

CÖHN, Heinz: Frieda Lindemeyer's cousin. He lived in Berlin and emigrated to the USA before World War II.

CÖHN, Richard and Mathilde: Frieda Lindemeyer's uncle who lived in Berlin until 1936 with Mathilde, his wife, and their son Günther. They then moved to Belgium, and Günther emigrated from there to South Africa. Richard was only able to follow him after the war, when his wife had already died.

COTTON, Mary: Edith's tutor at St Mary's. Having heard Edith express concern for her sister after the November 1938 pogrom, Mary Cotton's parents offered a guarantee to employ Eva-Maria as a household help, to assist her emigration to England.

D'AVIGDOR, Miss: employee at the Inter-Aid Committee in London.

DIENSTAG, Dr Paul: co-publisher and chief editor of *Geistiges Eigentum*, an international journal founded in 1935 in Leiden, Holland, which published articles on copyright law.

EDWARDS, Reverend: employee at Religious Film Ltd, to whom Georg Lindemeyer had applied for a job.

EPHRAIM, Kurt: emigrated with his parents and sister in May 1939. Their German citizenship was revoked in October 1939.

FINNIT, Mr: a Church of England priest in the Wiltshire parish where Wolfgang spent his summer with Mr Freer.

FRAULEIN GRETE: see LEWIN, Grete.

FREER, Mr: a Church of England priest in Chute, Wiltshire, who took Wolfgang in for the summer holidays in 1937.

GIGLI, Benjamino (1890–1957): the great Italian tenor.

GILES, Miss: warden of St Mary's Home, where Edith did her training in housekeeping.

GLÜCKSMANN family: Christians of Jewish origin who became close friends of the Lindemeyers. Professor Robert Glücksmann shared Georg Lindemeyer's intellectual interests. The youngest daughter, Gitta, was friends with Eva-Maria in Düsseldorf, and kept in contact with her after they had both emigrated to England in 1939. From 1934 onwards Robert Glücksmann suffered from Parkinson's disease.

GRANDMA: see HOBBIE, Mathilde.

GRÖNER, Fräulein: probably an employee of an English aid organisation.

GROSSMANN family: owners of the department store Alsberg & Co. Fritz Grossmann died at Buchenwald concentration camp, and his wife Martha was deported to Minsk with the Lindemeyers in November 1941. Their sons Gert and Werner had already left for England on a *Kindertransport* in May 1939.

GRÜNEBAUM family: probably relatives of the Lindemeyers from Wuppertal. Their son, Hermann, emigrated to England at the same time as Edith.

HAMACHER family: particularly close friends of the Lindemeyers whose son, Herbert, was also friends with Wolfgang.

Georg, Frieda and Eva-Maria hid in their flat during the night of the pogrom on 9–10 November 1938, and on the day of their deportation the Hamacher parents helped them to pack their last few belongings.

HEINIC family: Romanian in origin, they were neighbours of the Lindemeyer family until 1930. Leo Heinic died in February 1938, and their two sons left Germany before the Second World War. Rachela Heinic, a Christian of Jewish origin, was deported in April 1942 to Izbica, where she died.

HERZ, Elisabeth: her daughter Lore went to school with Edith in England. She returned to Düsseldorf in 1938 before emigrating with her parents to the USA.

HIRSCH, Ursula: employee at the Society of Friends, the Quaker organisation with its headquarters at Friends House in London.

HOBBIE, Mathilde: Georg Lindemeyer's mother.

HOBBIE, Dr Reinhard and Gertrud: Georg Lindemeyer's step-brother and stepsister-in-law.

HOHAUS, Frau: the Lindemeyers' long-time cleaning lady.

HOMANN, Pastor Rudolf and his wife: priest at the Johannes-kirche in Düsseldorf, who had a particularly close friendship with the Lindemeyers.

JANSENWIRTH, Hans: bookkeeper at Höllander, the Jewish import/export firm where Eva-Maria was also employed.

JUNG, Fräulein: teacher of French and Religious Education at the school in Düsseldorf attended by Eva-Maria and Edith.

KARTHAUS, Dr Werner and Hilde: a composer and friend of the Lindemeyers since before 1933.

KAUMANN family: this Catholic family were close friends of the Lindemeyers. Dr Heinz Kaumann was a lawyer with an insurance company in Düsseldorf.

KING, Miss: probably an employee of an English refugee organisation.

KLEINERTZ, Ilse: fellow student of Edith at St Mary's.

KÖHRMANN, Anneli: daughter of a Düsseldorf lawyer who went to school with Eva-Maria and Edith. Emigrated to Brazil before the war, along with many other lawyers' families from Düsseldorf.

LEIBHOLZ, Professor Gerhard: Jewish lawyer who taught at Göttingen University until he was forced to retire in 1938 because of his Jewish origins. He was married to Sabine Leibholz-Bonhoeffer (twin sister of Dietrich Bonhoeffer, the Protestant leader who actively opposed the Nazi regime and was executed for his involvement in the Resistance), and with her he emigrated to England in 1938. In 1947 he returned to Germany to resume his teaching at Göttingen, and later became a judge in the Federal Constitutional Court.

LEWIN, Grete: the Lindemeyers' housekeeper in Düsseldorf. Emigrated to England in 1935, where she married Paul Lewin (often referred to as Ellen, or Ilford, where they lived). Both were in close contact with the Lindemeyer children in England, and their friendship lasted until Grete Lewin's death in 1990.

LEWINSKY, Paul and Ilse: Frieda Lindemeyer's brother and sister-in-law. Lived in Berlin with their son Peter until 1934, when they emigrated to France. During the war the family hid in Mareuil (Vichy France). Only a few years later Paul and Ilse Lewinsky were killed in a car crash.

LION, Dr Hilde: emigrated to England in 1933, having been dismissed from her post in Germany for 'reasons of race'. Founder of the Stoatley Rough School, a mixed boarding school which was committed to educational reform, intended mainly for refugee children from Nazi Europe. It was recognised by the Ministry of Education in 1940. After the Second World War, a number of British pupils from disadvantaged backgrounds were sent to the school by local authorities. Stoatley Rough was run as a non-profit-making concern, and was closed upon the retirement of Dr Lion in 1960.

MENDEL and NEUBERGER: between 1933 and the pogrom in November 1938, these Jewish lawyers ran an office which gave advice on emigration issues.

MEYER, Bertha and Josef: Frieda's sister and brother-in-law who lived in Berlin with their son, Peter. They were deported to Riga in January 1942, where they both died.

PEARTREE, Tilly: a distant relative of Frieda Lindemeyer, living in Wiesbaden.

PERRY family: Eva-Maria lived with the family in London for a time upon her arrival in England.

PETERS, Ilse (also referred to as Ilse P.): Frieda Lindemeyer's closest friend. She was with them for the last night they spent in their apartment, and remained a friend of the Lindemeyer children after the war.

PHILIPPSOHN, Hanni (née Lewinsky) and Leo: Frieda Lindemeyer's eldest sister and her husband. Until 1933 she and her family lived in Dresden, where Leo owned a glass factory. After 1933 the family emigrated to Czechoslovakia and from there to Palestine, where her children still live.

POENSGEN, Fräulein: her exact identity cannot be established, but she was probably a teacher and a friend of Frieda Lindemeyer who helped with the process of Edith's emigration.

ROSEN, Herr: a friend of Wolfgang Lindemeyer.

ROSENSTEIN, Mrs: probably an employee of an English refugee organisation.

ROSENSTOCK, Frieda: a relative of Frieda Lindemeyer.

SCHLOSSMANN family: Margarete (née Bondi) and Professor Hans Schlossmann, emigrated from Germany together with their five children.

SCHOEN, Ruth (née Gnott): Eva-Maria's best friend at school, who stayed in contact with Frieda and Georg until their deportation. Also from a 'non-Ayran' family, she too was affected by National Socialist persecution. She remained a close friend of Eva Gilbert until the latter's death in 2005.

SCHWAB, Mrs: employee at the Inter-Aid Committee in London.

SPIERO, Heinrich: from September 1935 until Spring 1937 he was Chairman of the 'Reichsverband christlich deutscher Staatsbürger nichtarischer oder nicht rein arischer Abstammung e.V' (League of Christian German citizens of non-Aryan or not pure Aryan extraction), later known as the Paulusbund. From April 1937 onwards he ran the 'Buro Dr Heinrich Spiero' in Berlin, giving advice on emigration and other issues to Christians of Jewish origin. In pre-Hitler Germany he had also earned a reputation as a critic and historian of German literature.

SPONER, Fräulein: probably an employee of an English refugee organisation.

UNCLE ALFRED: see CÖHN, Dr Alfred and Martha.

UNCLE JOSI: see MEYER, Bertha and Josef.

UNCLE LEO: see PHILIPPSOHN, Hanni and Leo.

UNCLE PAUL: see LEWINSKY, Paul and Ilse.

UNCLE REINHARD: see HOBBIE, Dr Reinhard and Gertrud.

UNCLE RICHARD: see CÖHN, Richard and Mathilde.

WEGNER, Hilde (Hildegard): a close friend of Eva-Maria, also persecuted as a Christian of Jewish origin. She visited Frieda and Georg Lindemeyer regularly until a few days before they were deported.

WOLF, Dr Emmy: teacher of German language and literature at Stoatley Rough School. Emigrated to England in 1935.

A NOTE ON THE LINDEMEYERS

Georg Lindemeyer was born in 1887 in the Rhineland, Germany. He was educated in Bonn and Heidelberg universities and went on to become a successful lawyer in Düsseldorf. He was also a novelist, poet and critic and a scholar of law.

Frieda Lindemeyer was born in 1893 in Berlin. She married Georg Lindemeyer in 1915 and had three children with him: Eva-Maria, Edith and Wolfgang.

A NOTE ON THE EDITOR

Dr Christoph Moß is a researcher at the Krupp Historical Archive in Essen. He is a specialist on the German Jews of the National Socialist era. He has written many books and articles on the subject and edited the original, German edition of *A Thousand Kisses*.

A NOTE ON THE TRANSLATOR

Katharina Bielenberg has worked in publishing and more recently as a freelance editor and translator.